# THE NOBEL PRIZE
## ANNUAL
## 1989

# The Nobel Prize Annual 1989

IMG PUBLISHING • NEW YORK, NEW YORK

ISBN 0-9615344-9-4



Photography by Lars Aström

Cover and Interior Design by
Michaelis/Carpelis Design Assoc. Inc.
Project Editor: Kathleen Cahill

Printed in the United States of America

# CONTENTS

A *bust of Alfred Nobel.*

The Nobel Prizes annually focus world attention on a small number of men and women whose pursuit of excellence can be an inspiration for us all. *The Nobel Prize Annual 1989* will introduce you to the most recent prize winners to follow in this great tradition.

The 1989 prize recipients range from a religious leader who is also one of the world's great advocates of peaceful change to European and American scientists who have dedicated their lives to the search for fundamental knowledge. Their lives and personalities, their efforts, and their achievements are vividly presented in these pages.

Ernst & Young welcomes you to learn about the Nobel laureates and their work. As a firm, we celebrate the spirit of excellence embodied by Alfred Nobel, by the continuing influence of his Foundation, and by the prizes that bear his name.

*Ernst & Young*

*The 1989 Nobel laureates (front row) stand as the prize presentation ceremony begins.*

*The Nobel Prize presentation ceremony takes place in Stockholm's magnificent Concert Hall on December 10.*

# THE POWER OF THE WORD

**STIG RAMEL**
President of the Nobel Foundation

The Nobel Festival of 1989 was one of unusual optimism at which two laureates in Literature, Boris Pasternak and Camilo José Cela, made a special mark. When Boris Pasternak, who died in 1960, was awarded the Nobel Prize in Literature two years earlier, he first accepted the prize with pride and joy, but later declined under coercion by Soviet authorities. Today, the policies of glasnost and perestroika have helped change his government's attitudes toward Pasternak and his work. In fact, in anticipation of the one-hundredth anniversary (in 1990) of Pasternak's birth, a memorial exhibition was opened in Moscow in the autumn of 1989 with official approval.

But why should Pasternak not also be celebrated in Stockholm? And so the Nobel Foundation invited Pasternak's son Evgenij, who recently published a book about his father, to travel to Stockholm in 1989 to receive the gold medal his father could not accept thirty-one years earlier. On December 9, the traditional reception of the Nobel Foundation in honor of the Nobel laureates was made more memorable by the announcement that the Permanent Secretary of the Swedish Academy, Professor Sture Allén, would present a medal to Evgenij Pasternak. Beneath the glittering chandeliers of the Academy, a hushed crowd watched as Evgenij took his father's medal

*The novelist Camilo José Cela delivers a banquet speech before more than 1,000 guests.*

*Evgenij Pasternak (second from left) accepts the 1958 Nobel Prize in Literature in the name of his father, Boris Pasternak.*

into his hands. Five hundred guests were deeply moved by the simple ceremony that rectified a wrong made three decades earlier. Later, a Soviet journalist asked me if the Foundation should not change the text in its directory of laureates, which beneath Pasternak's name states: "Accepted first, later caused by the authorities of his country to decline the prize." The answer has to be "No, one shall not rewrite history." What happened in 1958 can not be undone. What we can do now is to honor a great Russian poet and remember his struggle for the freedom of literary creativity.

At the Nobel banquet the following eve-ning, the great Russian cellist Mstislav Rostropovitch played in Pasternak's honor. Maestro Rostropovitch and his wife Galina were close friends of the Pasternaks, and they were forced to leave their country during the Brezhnev years. For so many, 1989 will be remembered as a year when the wind of change and freedom turned the autumn of repression into the spring of liberty. Pasternak's gold medal was a small but significant symbol of that "December spring."

The Nobel Prize of 1989 to Camilo José Cela was also a reminder of the writer's task: to keep the light burning in the dark years of dictatorship and repression, as Cela did during the Franco years. His novels were written without regard for the regime of the day. Like Pasternak's *Doctor Zhivago*, some of his books had to be published first abroad before they were allowed in his own country. Like Pasternak, he fought political censorship and never gave in.

Now he came to Stockholm as the hero of his own people. To the Spaniard, he is "Don Camilo," author, actor, and TV personality of the first order, and his novel *The Family of Pascual Duarte* has been the most widely read in Spain since Cervantes' *Don Quixote*. Not unexpectedly, Cela's prize drew a great deal of attention in Spain: Spanish television sent a production crew to follow Cela during the Nobel festival, sending home daily broadcasts. King Juan Carlos was represented by his daughter, Infanta Doña Cristina, and the Spanish government was represented by its foreign minister.

A great number of Cela's friends and supporters joined his family to take part in the Nobel festival, including fifty friends from the small village of Galicia in northwestern Spain, where Cela was born seventy-three years ago.

The Nobel festival of 1989 was indeed one of optimism. The future looks somewhat brighter when a writer like Cela becomes a national hero and the injustice done to a man like Pasternak can be rectified. In recognizing Pasternak's greatness, the current leaders of the Soviet Union, which has given us so many writers of world importance, now allows its writers to live and be read without fear on both sides of the melting Iron Curtain.

The Swedish author August Strindberg once defiantly wrote in debate with one of the mighty of his time: "You have the power; I have the word; I have the power of the word." It is the power of this Spirit that we celebrate with Nobel and his laureates in Physics, Chemistry, Physiology or Medicine, Literature, and Peace.

# THE NOBEL PRIZE
## ANNUAL
## 1989

This portrait of Alfred Nobel hangs in the boardroom of the Nobel Foundation.

# CHAPTER 1

# NOBEL: THE MAN AND HIS LEGACY

**by Wilhelm Odelberg**
**Member of the Royal Swedish Academy of Sciences**

*By both nature and necessity Nobel was cosmopolitan, fluent in six languages and a man at home in most European capitals. He settled first in Hamburg, later and for the longest period in an elegant house in Paris, finally in his villa in Italy. The French writer Victor Hugo called him "the wealthiest vagabond in Europe."*

In 1907 the famous physicist Albert Abraham Michelson set off from America for the wilds of Stockholm to collect that year's Nobel Prize in physics. He took the Atlantic steamer from New York to Southampton, went by train to Harwich, from there to Esbjerg in Denmark, and so to Sweden. An English gentleman who boarded the boat at Harwich was given a seat at the same dining table as Michelson. During the voyage a somewhat heated discussion ensued between the two of them. The English gentleman spoke disparagingly of American science and military might—Michelson was on the teaching staff of the Annapolis Naval College—and Michelson in turn was critical of the exercise of power in the British Empire. They parted in the express hope of never setting eyes on one another again. But they did meet again, and sooner than either of them had expected. During the early years of the Nobel Prizes, up until World War I, few people were informed of the identity of the year's laureates before they appeared in the Banqueting Hall of the Royal Academy of Music to receive their prizes from the King of Sweden. So you can imagine the mutual astonishment of our two fighting cocks on discovering that they both were Nobel laureates, the English gentleman being one Rudyard Kipling. Michelson's granddaughter, who includes this anecdote in a biography of her grandfather, is unable to tell us whether Kipling and Michelson were reconciled afterward. In any event, this was neither the first nor the last instance of a Nobel Prize generating controversy.

When the first Nobel Prize in Literature came up in 1901, the literary world expected one of the current giants of literature to be selected for the honor. They were wrong. The Nobel Committee of the Swedish Academy chose the French author Sully Prudhomme "in special recognition of his poetic composition, which gives evidence of lofty idealism, artistic perfection, and a rare combination of qualities of both heart and intellect." Sully Prudhomme was unquestionably a brilliant poet, but his true fame was forty years past. Young writers in Sweden were furious with the Academy, and a letter signed by many of Sweden's most eminent authors was sent to Leo Tolstoy, deploring the fact that he had not been made the first recipient. The task of the Swedish Academy, of course, is a difficult one. And so, not infrequently, the choice falls on somebody who is not well known to the general public, thereby confounding all manner of conjecture. Graham Greene, for example, has been rumored to be the front-runner on several occasions when in fact that distinction fell to some less famous Greek, Italian, or Japanese writer. The choice of laureate in literature has often been criticized in literary journals and newspapers. Prizes have also had political ramifications. For instance, the 1958 Prize in Literature went to the Soviet author Boris Pasternak "for his important achievement both in contemporary lyrical poetry and the field of the great Russian epic tradition." For ideological reasons that are not altogether clear, Pasternak was out of

*Rudyard Kipling.*

favor with the regime at the time and was forced to decline the prize. Today, twenty-nine years after his death, he has been restored to grace and his works are once more being printed in the Soviet Union.

When the 1953 Prize in Literature went to Sir Winston Churchill "for his mastery of historical and biographical description as well as for his brilliant oratory in defending exalted human values," some critics felt that the distinction ought to have gone to a fiction writer instead. But many others welcomed this tribute to civilization. When, in

1970, the Prize in Literature went to Alexander Solzhenitsyn "for the ethical force with which he has pursued the indispensable traditions of Russian literature," the choice was yet another that did not go down well with the Soviet government. His autobiography and Nobel Lecture were secretly conveyed out of the country for publication in the yearbook of the Nobel Foundation. But several years were to elapse before the laureate, exiled from his native country, was able to collect his prize in Stockholm.

The Nobel Prizes in Physics, in Chemistry, and in Physiology or Medicine have come in for less criticism. But some scathing remarks have been made on occasions, for example, in the journals *Nature* and *Science*. I remember that when Sir Martin Ryle and Antony Hewish from Cambridge, England, shared the prize for their remarkable discoveries in astrophysics, it was said that one of the most vital contributions had been made by an assistant at the observatory whom the Nobel Committee had overlooked.

The most controversial prize of all, of course, has been the Nobel Peace Prize, awarded by the Norwegian Nobel Committee. The prize has often gone to organizations (or representatives of organizations) that have played an important part in the pursuit of peace. Quite naturally, the first recipient in this category, in 1901, was Henri Dunant, founder of the International Red Cross.

On quite a number of occasions the Peace Prize has gone to people in the political limelight who have irked the wielders of power, but campaigned for human dignity and reconciliation. The first startling in-stance came when the 1935 Peace Prize was awarded (in 1936) to the German Carl von Ossietzky, a radical pacifist and journalist. He was imprisoned in one of Hitler's concentration camps, and the Führer was so enraged by the decision that he forbade any Germans to accept Nobel Prizes in the future. The Nobel Committee, unmoved, persistently awarded prizes to Germans.

Other peace laureates have caused tempers to flare in one place or another: Martin Luther King; Andrei Sakharov; President Anwar Sadat of Egypt and Prime Minister Menachem Begin of Israel, who shared a prize; Lech Walesa; and Archbishop Desmond Tutu, to mention but a few examples.

Sweden and Norway do not often attract attention in the international press. A remarkable exception to this rule is the announcement of the year's Nobel Prizes, usually made in October, and the events surrounding the award ceremony on December 10. It is only natural then that interest be directed also at the man who was the cause of all that attention.

Alfred Nobel was very much an international figure. He was born in Stockholm in 1833; grew up in St. Petersburg, Russia; lived the greater part of his life in Paris; and died in San Remo, Italy, in 1896.

Even at an early age, he began to take an interest in the explosives industry. After studies in various countries, he founded, in 1864, Nitroglycerin AB and set up factories outside Stockholm and Hamburg. Since liquid nitroglycerine proved to be extremely dangerous to transport, Nobel set about producing a more stable explosive and in 1866 he invented dynamite, which is produced by mixing nitroglycerine and kieselguhr, or fossil meal. A subsequent improvement on this was explosive gelatin, invented by Nobel in 1875.

In 1893 Nobel began to take an interest in the Swedish arms industry, establishing himself at Bofors, in the Värmland district of western Sweden. During the closing period of his life he annually visited Karlskoga, where he had a manor known as Björkborn. A large research laboratory was also set up in Karlskoga for the study, above all, of smokeless gunpowder, or Nobel powder. Numerous engineers were employed at this laboratory, including Ragnar Sohlman, who later became managing director of the Nobel Foundation.

Nobel was also responsible for real inventions in a variety of other fields, including artificial silk and leather and gutta-percha. He registered no less than three hundred and fifty-five patents in different countries. In 1983 the manor of Björkborn and the old laboratory nearby were converted into a museum to mark the sesquicentenary of Alfred Nobel's birth. The laboratory has been reconstructed as it was in Nobel's day. The manor now houses the greater part of Nobel's personal library.

Through his inventions, mainly in the field of explosives, and the revenues from the companies he founded, Nobel amassed a considerable fortune, yet he lived a simple life. He was unmarried, and posterity's eager delvings into his relationships have given fairly scanty results. His emotional life was sublimated in favor of new inventions. To him, a day without any new ideas taking shape was a day wasted. "But," he said "if only a few out of a hundred such ideas ever bear fruit, I consider I have gained a rich result." Nobel clearly had an unusual capacity for work. He spoke and wrote six languages, and was an extremely witty correspondent. He received, of course, numerous honors.

On November 25, 1895, Nobel drew up his will in Paris. There has been a great deal of speculation as to Nobel's thoughts before he made his final wishes known. He had corresponded a great deal over the years with the well-known Austrian author and apostle of peace Bertha von Suttner, which probably gave him the inspiration for what was to be the Nobel Peace Prize.

Nobel had two brothers, Ludvig and Robert, who settled in Russia and developed, with great success, the oil finds in Baku on the Caspian Sea. They, too, became extremely wealthy and have been called "the Russian Rockefellers." Alfred Nobel had some interests in the Russian companies headed by his brother Ludvig, who died in Cannes, France, in 1888. When the French press reported his death a paper in Paris confused Ludvig with Alfred and ran the headline LE MARCHAND DE LA MORT EST MORT—THE MERCHANT OF DEATH IS DEAD. We can assume that Alfred Nobel, faced with this headline, wondered whether this was the sort of obituary he would get when his own time came.

Anyway, without really discussing the matter with anyone—he had been disappointed by lawyers before and decided not to employ one this time—Nobel drew up his will and deposited it in a bank in Stockholm. Its contents were surprising to his relatives,

A *young Alfred Nobel.*

colleagues, and the general public in Sweden:

The whole of my remaining realizable estate shall be dealt with in the following way:

The capital shall be invested by my executors in safe securities and shall constitute a fund, the interest on which shall be distributed in the form of prizes to those who, during the preceding year, shall have conferred the greatest benefit on mankind. The said interest shall be divided into five equal parts, which shall be apportioned as follows: one part of the person who shall have made the most important discovery or invention within the field of physics; one part to the person who shall have made the most important chemical discovery or improvement; one part to the person who shall have made the most important discovery within the domain of physiology or medicine; one part to the person who shall have produced in the field of literature the most outstanding work of an idealistic tendency; and one part to the person who shall have done the most or the best work for the fraternity among nations, for the abolition or reduction of standing armies, and for the holding and promotion of peace congresses.

The prizes for physics and chemistry shall be awarded by the Swedish Academy of Sciences; that for physiology or medical works by the Karolinska Institute in Stockholm; that in literature by the Academy in Stockholm; and that for champions of peace by a committee of five persons to be elected by the Norwegian Storting [Parliament].[*] It is my express wish that in awarding the prizes no consideration whatever shall be given to the nationality of the candidates, so that the most worthy shall receive the prize, whether he be a Scandinavian or not.

His relatives were quite naturally disappointed. Many people regarded the will as

---

[*] In 1905 when the Union of Sweden and Norway was dissolved, it was decided that the Norwegian Nobel Committee would have the task of adjudicating and awarding the Peace Prize. Its five members are appointed by the Norwegian Storting but it should be noted that the Committee acts entirely on its own, independent of the Storting.

*A photograph of Nobel's laboratory in San Remo.*

reflecting a lack of patriotic feeling. The French state, for its part, was keenly interested in the question of whether Alfred Nobel's fortune had its legal domicile in France or Sweden. (What decided the issue was that Nobel had transferred to Sweden his famous Orloff carriage horses. By French custom, wherever the carriage horses were, there the estate inventory had to be drafted.)

## CHOOSING LAUREATES

There were thus five Nobel Prizes, and there are now six, if we count the Alfred Nobel Memorial Prize in Economics added in 1968. Since the Nobel Foundation's capital was acquired more than eighty years ago, it has grown to around 1.7 billion Swedish kronor (Skr), corresponding to approximately $261 million. The prize sum in 1989 was Skr 3 million, or $460,000. Given inflation, taxes, and other burdens, however, this growth is illusory. When the first prize was awarded the figure was Skr 150,000, and corresponded to twenty years' salary for a university professor. If the same were true today, the prize sum would have to be Skr 4.9 million, or about $799,000.

By the terms of the Nobel Foundation's

statutes, a prize can be equally divided between two achievements or awarded jointly to two or more persons for work that they have done together. The Peace Prize can also be awarded to an institution or association. In any given year, all prizes are of the same amount. Yet they vary in size from year to year, depending on the yield of the fund from which they are drawn. That it has been possible to increase the yield in step with inflation is owing largely to the fact that the Nobel Foundation is not tax-exempt and therefore escapes the capital gains tax that has been such a burden in all capital administration in Sweden.

By the terms of the statutes, proposals shall be submitted prior to February 1 of the year in which the award is to be made. Previous laureates and the officials and members of academies, universities, and scientific institutions throughout the world are all entitled to nominate candidates. Decisions are normally made by the Swedish award bodies between October 1 and November 15. The Norwegian Nobel Committee makes its decision on the Peace Prize between September 1 and November 15.

Traditionally, the Nobel Prizes are presented with due ceremony in Stockholm and Oslo on December 10, Nobel Day, the anniversary of Alfred Nobel's death. Apart from the monetary prize, each laureate receives a diploma and a gold medal of generous size (the gold is currently valued at $3,000). In Sweden the practice is for the King to award the prizes in the Stockholm Concert Hall, after which a banquet is held for some thirteen hundred people in the Stockholm City Hall. In Oslo the Peace Prize is presented by

the chairman of the Norwegian Nobel Committee, traditionally in the presence of the royal family. By the terms of the statutes, a laureate is required within six months of the award ceremony to give a "Nobel Lecture"; this is usually delivered on acceptance of the prize.

Work on the election of laureates continues practically all year round. The committees for the various prizes are required to take previous proposals into consideration and to note new proposals. In 1988, nominations for prizes numbered two hundred and three for Physics, two hundred and seventy-seven for Chemistry, one hundred and eighty-five for Physiology or Medicine, one hundred and twenty-nine for Literature, one hundred and eighty-nine for Peace, and eighty-one for Economic Sciences. Naturally, a lot of these nominations recur from year to year.

Discussions usually arise in regard to awarding the prize to a team of researchers for a single discovery. It may be, for example, that candidate A has made a remarkable research finding but the significance of the finding was first established by candidate B and the discovery was then decisively developed by candidate C. The question can then be put as follows: Is candidate A to receive the entire award? If this is thought inappropriate, should the prize be split into three equal parts? No more than three laureates may be elected in the same subject.

Interest in the Nobel Prizes extends beyond the current awards. Interest in the history of science has increased enormously in Europe and America since World War II, and numerous chairs in this subject have

*The 1989 laureates meet at the Swedish Academy. Front (left to right): Norman Ramsey, Camilo José Cela, Trygve Haavelmo. Second Row: Michael Bishop, Sidney Altman, Harold Varmus, Thomas Cech, Wolfgang Paul, Hans Dehmelt.*

been established.

There is a touch of flamboyant gesture about Nobel's will as he casts his millions into the air, without inquiring too closely where they are going to land. The main thing was that they should not get into the pockets of his legal heirs. This massive donation was probably one of innumerable ideas, and Nobel's imagination seems to have been prolific at the time his will was drawn up. He oscillated from phonographs and telephones to projectiles of various kinds. He simply did not have time to work out his ideas in more detail, and his last will and testament, like several of his provisional patent applications, remained an evanescent sketch.

Of one thing, however, we can be relatively certain: it was people with ideas he wanted to reward, people with inspiration. In other words, people of his own kind. This is why the prizes had to refer to achievements during the past year. There is no Nobel Prize in Technology, because Nobel knew from his own experience that a successful invention is often rewarded through the patent system. But a medical or chemical discovery is something different; there is nothing to guarantee that the person making the discovery will have a share in the resultant profit.

Although interest in the Nobel Prizes has fluctuated with the years, they have become internationally established in the way Alfred Nobel intended. They are astonishingly well known in large parts of the world. Interest in Alfred Nobel personally has also been sustained, perhaps partly because he was such an unusual personality. There is no formula or slogan with which he can be pinned down.

*Wilhelm Odelberg, Ph.D., is former head librarian of Stockholm University, a member of the Royal Swedish Academy of Sciences, and vice president of the Royal Academy of Military Sciences. He is author of several books and articles on modern history, biographies, and the history of science, and editor (1968–1988) of* Les Prix Nobel, *the yearbook of the Nobel Foundation.*

*Carl von Ossietzky.*

# CHAPTER 2

# CARL von OSSIETZKY RETROSPECTIVE

**by Irwin Abrams**

*"In one moment the conscience of the world arose, and the name which it spoke was his."*
*In celebration of the 100th anniversary of the birth of Carl von Ossietzky, winner of the 1935 Nobel Prize in Peace*

In October 1989, Germans on both sides of the Berlin Wall celebrated the one-hundredth birthday of a Nobel Peace Prize winner who had been martyred for his opposition to Hitler. Carl von Ossietzky (1889–1938), the courageous antimilitarist editor, was thrown into a concentration camp when the Nazis came into power and so cruelly mistreated that he was already marked for death when finally released.

While both East and West German governments have recognized Ossietzky as a hero for his struggle against National Socialism, the East Berlin masses who brought down the wall in November were acting far more in keeping with Ossietzky's free-thinking democratic spirit than their government ever had.

In 1936 the Oslo Nobel Committee, in a display of Norwegian courage and independence, awarded the Peace Prize to Ossietzky, despite threats from the Third Reich. At a time when Hitler was being treated with respect and even sympathy by some European statesmen, this was a stinging moral defeat for the Führer.

In retrospect, this award to a concentration camp victim represents the first human rights award ever made by the Norwegian Committee. It was the forerunner of much later awards as those to Andrei Sakharov, Lech Walesa, and Desmond Tutu. Moreover, the organized effort to generate widespread support for Ossietzky was a precedent for the work now carried on in behalf of prisoners of conscience by Amnesty International, also a Nobel Peace Prize winner. And in 1989 the prize for the Dalai Lama was in large part a recognition of his struggle to defend the human rights of the Tibetan people.

The campaign for Ossietzky was organized by a small band of refugees from Nazi

*Von Ossietzky pictured in 1932 with his daughter, Rosalinda.*



Germany who mobilized world opinion through an international network of fellow émigrés. One of these was Willy Brandt, who would himself win the Nobel Peace Prize in 1971 as Chancellor of the Federal Republic of Germany. On that occasion Brandt declared the Ossietzky prize "a victory over barbarism. I should like to express today to the Nobel Committee a belated thanks in the name of a free Germany."

Brandt was not wrong to see the award in historical perspective as "a victory over barbarism," but this was not the way the committee saw it at the time. At the 1936 award ceremony the committee chairman, Fredrik Stang, declared that the award for Ossietzky was for "his valuable contribution to the cause of peace—nothing more, and certainly nothing less."

Of course, we can never know exactly what took place in the conference room of the Nobel Committee when the decision was reached on November 23 of that year. No minutes are ever taken of the discussions, and the members are pledged to silence. There are, however, records from all the major actors in the drama; the campaign organizers, the Nazi authorities, even Ossietzky himself. In fact, we probably know more about this award than any other Nobel Peace Prize.

Until the campaign began, few outside Germany had heard about Ossietzky. In 1931 had he been briefly on the pages of the world press, when, as editor of the radical weekly *Die Weltbühne*, he was convicted on a trumped-up charge of treason for publishing information about Germany's secret rearmament. He had been attacking every sign of revived militarism in the Weimar Republic so effectively with his eloquent and ironic pen that the Reichswehr generals had determined to silence him.

He refused to flee abroad, saying that to fight for his ideals, his place was in Germany and that his voice would sound hollow from beyond its borders. Released by a Christmas amnesty after serving six months, he returned to his editorial desk and again took up his attacks against the Nazis. When Hitler became chancellor, Ossietzky again refused to leave the country, and he was soon arrested, along with other leading opponents of the regime, and sent to prison and then to a concentration camp.

In November 1935 a representative of the International Red Cross Committee was permitted to visit him in the concentration camp of Esterwegen and found a "trembling deadly pale something, a creature that appeared to be without feeling, one eye swollen, teeth knocked out, it dragged a broken, badly healed leg . . . a human being that had reached the uttermost limits of what could be borne."

Ossietzky's friends who had fled Germany learned about his pitiful condition from released fellow prisoners and vainly sought his release. They finally hit upon the idea of drawing world attention to his plight by having him nominated for the Nobel Peace Prize. They did not expect that he would win it, but they hoped that the pressure of public opinion might force the Nazis to stop his mistreatment and perhaps even to let him go free.

The leadership was taken by Hellmut von Gerlach, former *Weltbühne* editor, who was head of the German League of the Rights of Man in Paris. Assisted by the journalists Hilde Walter and Milly Zirker and the former law student Konrad Reisner, Gerlach set up an international network of German émigrés to recruit for Ossietzky's cause some of the most eminent men and women of the day. The network included, among others, Kurt Grossman in Prague; Rudolf Olden and Ernst Toller in London; Willy Brandt, strategically situated in Oslo; and Otto Nathan and Albert Einstein in the United States. When Gerlach died in August 1935, Hilde Walter took over, working night and day,

financially supported by her friend Otto Nathan, a distinguished economist and confidant of Einstein.

The Paris group was careful to remain in the background, fearing that if the Nazis learned that the campaign was being organized by political refugees, not only would there be no chance that the publicity would bring Ossietzky better conditions, but it might even result in reprisals against him by

*Two of his friends escorted von Ossietzky as he entered a Nazi prison camp in 1933.*

15

*T*estifying (center) at his trial in a Leipzig courtroom.



his jailers. Consequently, Einstein enlisted the help of Jane Addams, who as a winner of the Nobel Peace Prize (1931) was qualified to nominate Ossietzky, which she did in a cable to Oslo. Other distinguished public figures who agreed to help in this way were Professors Harold Laski of the London School of Economics and André Philip of the University of Lyons.

Gerlach now sought advice from Nobel Committee member Christian Lange, whom he had met when Lange was Secretary-General of the Interparliamentary Union. Lange discreetly wrote in reply that he could only speak about "procedure," but the procedure he advised was crucial in Ossietzky's winning the prize. Lange warned Gerlach not to argue that the prize might bring Ossietzky freedom but to submit a well-substantiated proposal emphasizing his work for peace.

This is exactly what Gerlach did, accompanying his nomination with a memorandum on Ossietzky's life and work, with quotations from his articles and statements in his behalf from prominent intellectuals and politicians testifying that Ossietzky had made *Die Weltbühne* the Weimar Republic's most influential voice against war and militarism and for international understanding. After all the nominations had reached Oslo, Gerlach and his friends began to feed information about the distinguished nominators to European and American newspapers. But Willy Brandt reported from Oslo that few people had heard of Ossietzky and there was little hope for his candidacy.

However, from Gestapo documents discovered after the war, we know that this publicity worried the Nazi authorities. Beginning in 1934, German diplomats reported proposals for an Ossietzky peace prize as part of their regular coverage of anti-Nazi sentiments in the press. The diplomats were told to report that Ossietzky's annual physical examinations showed him to be in good health. The superficiality of these checkups is demonstrated by one report of the concentration camp doctor that he had found evidence of a heart ailment but had no question about Ossietzsky's *Haftfähigkeit* ("imprisonability").

When the members of the Nobel Committee met in Oslo to discuss the prize for 1935, they had before them a strong recommendation for Ossietzky from committee adviser Wilhelm Keilhau. Keilhau clearly based his report largely on Gerlach's memorandum. He quoted with approval the famous French writer Romain Rolland's letter to the committee declaring that it "has never yet had the opportunity to crown an apostle of peace steadfast unto martyrdom." But the committee announced on November 19 that it would postpone awarding the 1935 prize until 1936. Committee member Halvdan Koht, Norway's foreign minister, being a historian, could not resist making a note of the fact that no one had spoken for Ossietzky.

The next day, an event took place in Oslo that suddenly popularized Ossietzky and completely changed the situation. On November 20 there appeared in two conservative newspapers an attack on Ossietzky by the great Norwegian writer Knut Hamsun, in his old age a strong supporter of the Third Reich. His attack led fellow writers, students, liberal and labor groups, and even some conservatives to declare their solidarity with the persecuted prisoner who could not defend himself. Working together with Mimi Sverdrup Lunden, an energetic worker for peace and women's rights, Willy Brandt found increasing opportunities to place pro-Ossietzky articles and to arrange for the lobbying of Nobel Committee members.

In Paris, Walter and her colleagues worked hard to secure nominations before the February 1 deadline. She compiled a very impressive memorandum: it included essays by Heinrich Mann and Konrad Heiden; a letter to the London *Times* from Wickham Steed, the noted British publicist; the letters to the Nobel Committee from Thomas Mann and Einstein; and a model letter of nomination. Twenty copies were sent to qualified nominators in nine countries for further distribution.

In Switzerland, Dr. Hans Oprecht, a member of the National Council, circulated his copy in the Swiss Parliament and sent it to Oslo signed by over half of the Swiss parliamentarians, representing seven parties. In Paris, Milly Zirker's French translation was signed by one hundred and twenty-one deputies and thirteen professors. Willy Brandt put the memorandum to good use in Oslo, where the Labor Party decided formally to support Ossietzky. In Stockholm fifty-nine Socialist deputies jointly signed a nomination. In England a pamphlet was published over the names of such leading personalities as Bertrand Russell, Aldous Huxley, H. G. Wells, Professor G. P. Gooch, Norman Angell, Gilbert Murray, and Leonard and Virginia Woolf. By the deadline a record eighty-six nominations from eleven countries had been submitted, many of them representing groups of signers.

The publicity alarmed the Nazi government, which was preparing for the Berlin Olympic Games and the great propaganda show of the "new Germany" that was to be made there. A Gestapo report of May 22, 1936, noted the extraordinary interest shown abroad in the Ossietzky nomination and the continuing inquiries about the state of his health from such sources as the Quaker representatives in Berlin, the International Red Cross, and the government of the United States. The Gestapo never discovered that these inquiries were often inspired by the émigré network. The result was a more thorough physical examination of Ossietzky, whose condition was found to be so serious that "one day his sudden decease must be reckoned on."

Now the Nazis had to worry about the bad publicity that would follow his death in the concentration camp. Should they release him? A Gestapo memorandum of April 3 argued against this, declaring that he would be used as "a star witness against National Socialist Germany." So the authorities de-

cided to keep him in camp, but to give him better medical care, which was to be well documented, in order to answer the agitation that could be expected if he died.

But this course must have seemed too risky, and on May 23 Goering ordered that Ossietzky be transferred from the camp to the prison wing of the Virchow Hospital in Berlin. With Ossietzky's release from the concentration camp, the campaign organizers had won their first victory. The ill treatment of their friend was now ended, but the doctors at the hospital diagnosed open-lung tuberculosis and declared that the pa-

*P*risoner 562.

tient would only get worse in confinement. Goering apparently felt that the Nazis would now be adequately covered if Ossietzky were to die in a hospital; there was no need to reveal that measures were taken to keep him well guarded. So Ossietzky was left at Virchow.

Meanwhile, to counter the growing public support for Ossietzky, German propagandists and diplomats distributed material about the "traitor Ossietzky" and promoted Baron Coubertin, founder of the modern Olympic games as a potential laureate. Goebbels spoke with heavy sarcasm in a radio speech about people who want to give Nobel Peace Prizes to traitors. And in September his Propaganda ministry got a Danish newspaper to publish an account of a supposed interview with Ossietzky in the hospital, in which he was said to have changed his mind about National Socialism and even to have bade farewell to the interviewer with a "Heil Hitler!" Almost all the foreign journalists in Berlin dismissed the story as a fabrication.

However, Professor Frede Castberg, the Nobel Committee adviser in international law who had been assigned to write the report on Ossietzky, was very thorough and conscientious, and while he had been impressed by the volume of supporting material on Ossietzky that he had plowed through, this seemed one more question that needed to be answered: was there any truth at all in the report of the interview? There were two other persistent questions: had Ossietzky accepted money from foreign governments in opposing the secret rearmament as some other German pacifists had done, and what

about Communist claims that Ossietzky was a supporter of the Soviet Union?

To answer these questions, Castberg, in a most unusual move, asked Hilde Walter to meet him on September 26 in Geneva, where he would be meeting with the League of Nations Assembly. He would need irrefutable evidence if he were to recommend Ossietzky to the committee. Walter could speak from personal knowledge as to Ossietzky's absolute integrity and his critical attitude toward Communism. He was a free spirit, not a party man, and he had found much to criticize on the Left as well as on the Right. Walter remained in Geneva for a week, collecting in the League library documentation from Ossietzky writings to send to Oslo. One week before the committee was to meet, Walter was able to supplement this with indirect word from Ossietzky himself denying that any such interview had taken place.

In Berlin the Nazi authorities had to recognize that their invented interview had failed to halt the surge of public support for Ossietzky. In the first week of November they released him from Virchow so that if he were granted the prize, they could represent it abroad as proof that he was a free man. The Quaker representative in Berlin arranged for him to be admitted to the private Westend Hospital, but Goering ordered that strict surveillance by the Gestapo was to be continued and Ossietzky's whereabouts were still to be kept secret.

Hilde Walter heard of Ossietzky's whereabouts from Hedwig Hünicke, the former *Weltbühne* staffer who had remained in Berlin and had been allowed by the Gestapo to transmit to Ossietzky the funds that came

*Carl von Ossietzky in Papenburg-Esterwegen concentration camp in 1934.*

through the Quakers and now to visit him. Walter immediately sent word to Mimi Sverdrup Lunden, who told Nobel Committee member Lange on November 13. He received the news "with joy and surprise," Lunden reported to Walter, and when she remarked that surely the Committee would not be as opposed to a free man as to a state prisoner, Lange "only smiled, but his eyes were sharp." At his request, Lunden telegraphed Walter to find out exactly where Ossietzky was, which is how the committee knew where to reach him when they finally decided to give him the prize.

A change in the composition of the committee had further enhanced Ossietzky's chances. On November 9 Halvdan Koht notified his fellow members that as foreign minister he felt he should not participate in the upcoming meeting to consider the 1935 and 1936 awards. Obviously, if the foreign minister sat on a committee that gave the prize to Ossietzky, Germany would hold the Norwegian government responsible.

Koht's withdrawal was followed by that of the leader of the bourgeois party of the Left and former foreign minister, and the two were replaced by their alternates, a conservative attorney and a Labor Party leader who supported Ossietzky as editor of its newspaper. The committee had now gained an advocate for Ossietzky and lost two members who had opposed him in 1935.

Another factor may have favored the Ossietzky candidacy. Even though the German minister had been informed that the Nobel Committee was quite independent of the Norwegian government, on November 19 he was instructed to warn Norway that a prize for Ossietzky would be considered as an anti-German demonstration and could have grave consequences. When, only four days later, the members of the committee convened to reach their decision, they had to take this threat seriously. But it is just possible that this heavy-handed German gesture may actually have served to cause these patriotic Norwegians to get their backs up.

The Nobel Committee had received the advisory report from Professor Castberg, which was a strong recommendation for Ossietzky. There was abundant documentation of Ossietzky's crusade for peace from the columns of *Die Weltbühne*, evidently supplied by Walter from her research in Geneva, just the kind of substantiation Lange had advised Gerlach to provide.

We can only conjecture how the discussion went. Presumably Tranmael argued for Ossietzky, supported by Lange, whom Lunden had found so sympathetic to her efforts. Bernhard Hanssen, a conservative shipping magnate who was a leader in the organized peace movement, had not favored Ossietzky in 1935, but he was bound to have been influenced by the many nominations from members of the Council of the International Peace Bureau, which Walter had rounded up.

But what caused Stang to change his mind? Years later Castberg told Brandt that Stang had always had his doubts about the Ossietzky prize. He was a conservative, but a strong champion of intellectual liberty, which he emphasized in his speech at the award ceremony. He began by saying that Ossietzky belonged to no political party, that he seemed to be a "liberal of the old school," which to Stang meant having "a burning love for freedom of thought and expression; a firm belief in free competition in all spiritual fields; a broad international outlook; a respect for values created by other nations—and all of these dominated by the theme of peace." These were the values held by Stang himself, as well as by other members of the Nobel Committee. Stang also said he had been impressed by the flood of

*After receiving the Nobel Prize, von Ossietzky (seated) was interviewed by newspapermen in a hospital, where he was recovering following his release from prison.*

letters of support for Ossietzky, for which the émigré network was largely responsible.

However the discussion went, the committee agreed to grant the postponed 1935 prize to Ossietzky and then decided on a more conventional choice for 1936, Foreign Minister Saavedra Lamas of Argentina, who had made important contributions to peace in Latin America.

The committee telegram was delivered to Ossietzky on the same day, November 23, in the Westend Hospital. We can try to imagine his feelings: astonishment, disbelief, gratitude, apprehension that the news might bring reprisals. It was not until November

October 1989. Artist Klaus Simon works on a sculpture commemorating von Ossietzky's 100th birthday.

28 that Ossietzky replied in a brief telegram of acceptance: "Thankful for undeserved honor."

What had delayed this reply was the pressure the Gestapo was applying to get Ossietzky to reject the prize. He was even summoned to an interview with Goering. But Ossietzky held firm, and he stated his reasons on a torn piece of paper, dated November 26, which has been preserved. He wrote:

> After careful consideration I have decided to accept the Nobel Peace Prize. I do not share the view expressed by representatives of the [Gestapo] that in so doing I am excluding myself from the German *Volksgemeinschaft*. . . . I am also moved to accept the prize by the circumstance that a rejection could be misunderstood. It could be maintained that I had done this under pressure, which would lead to new protest actions. There has arisen abroad, as far as I can judge, an "Ossietzky Affair." Acceptance brings it to an end, rejection keeps it going.

On the same day that he sent his acceptance to Oslo, four foreign correspondents were permitted to hold a brief interview with Ossietzky in the hospital in the presence of a representative of the Propaganda Ministry. Ossietzky, pale and wan, took care not to offend the authorities in his remarks, but he declared, "I was and I remain a pacifist." He hoped to go to Oslo to receive the prize and to give a Nobel Lecture on the "Coexistence of Peoples." He hoped that no ill would befall Norway because of his acceptance.

On November 25 the German minister in

Oslo had notified the Norwegian government that his government regarded the award to a notorious traitor as an insulting provocation and would reserve to itself the consequence to be drawn. The only consequence of any significance, however, was Hitler's decree at the end of January forbidding Germans in the future to accept a Nobel Prize in any field. The story that the Germans took reprisals against members of the Nobel Committee during their occupation of Norway in World War II has no basis in fact.

The German government always claimed that Ossietzky was a free man and could have gone to Oslo to receive the prize if his health permitted. The Gestapo documents reveal, however, that he was refused permission to leave the country because of his stated pacifism. To the Nazis this meant that as soon as he was beyond the border he would engage in anti-German propaganda, and he would have the Nobel Prize money to help him do it. The documents also show that the Gestapo objected when Ossietzky moved on December 12 to a private sanatorium in northern Berlin, because it was harder to guard him there.

So the award ceremony in Oslo on December 10 went on without Ossietzky and also without King Haakon, who traditionally attended, but on this occasion was thought to be displeased with the decision, as were many Norwegian conservatives.

As for Ossietzky, he lived out his last months isolated from the world in the drab, meager surroundings of the sanatorium, where at least his wife was allowed to share his tiny room and to watch over him lovingly

Von Ossietzky (standing 3rd from left) in the concentration camp.

in the last stages of his painful illness. Most of the prize money was embezzled by a crooked lawyer who may have been a creature of the Gestapo. Ossietzky died on May 4, 1938, and the Gestapo, true guardians of the "New Germany," saw to it that his ashes were buried in secret.

Elsewhere news of Ossietzky's death brought lead editorials praising him as a fallen fighter for peace and freedom. Thomas Mann anticipated that "the figure of this brave and pure-minded journalist could grow in time to a fighter for humanity and a martyr of legendary proportions." Heinrich Mann perhaps best summed up in a few words the meaning of the campaign for Ossietzky's Peace Prize: "In one moment the conscience of the world arose, and the name which it spoke was his."

NOTE

*This essay was adapted from a paper presented at the Joint Annual Meeting of the British and United States International Studies Associations in London, England, March 1989. Chief sources were the campaign correspondence of Hilde Walter at the International Institute for Social History, Amsterdam; the Nobel Committee archives, Oslo; the Ossietzky Collection at the University of Oldenburg; and interviews with the surviving members of the Gerlach network, Willy Brandt and Konrad Reisner.*

# NOBEL WEEK 1989

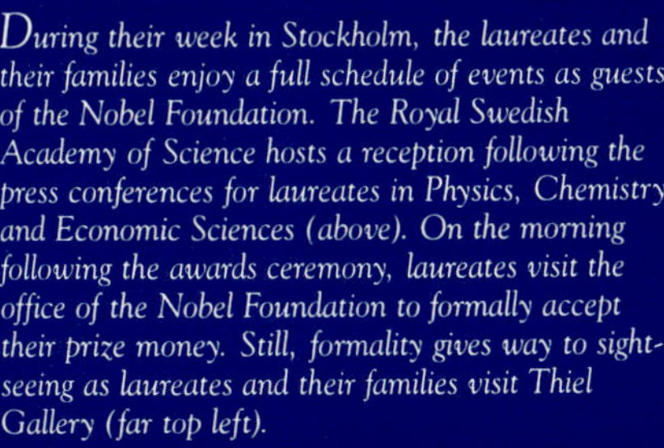

During their week in Stockholm, the laureates and their families enjoy a full schedule of events as guests of the Nobel Foundation. The Royal Swedish Academy of Science hosts a reception following the press conferences for laureates in Physics, Chemistry and Economic Sciences (above). On the morning following the awards ceremony, laureates visit the office of the Nobel Foundation to formally accept their prize money. Still, formality gives way to sightseeing as laureates and their families visit Thiel Gallery (far top left).

*The Nobel Prize laureates Ramsey, Dehmelt and Paul.*

26

# CHAPTER 3

# THE NOBEL PRIZE IN PHYSICS

## THE WORK OF PROFESSOR NORMAN F. RAMSEY, PROFESSOR HANS G. DEHMELT, PROFESSOR DR. WOLFGANG PAUL

*The works of the laureates have led to dramatic advances in the field of precision spectroscopy in recent years. Methods have been developed that form the basis for our present definition of time, and these techniques are applied for such disparate purposes as testing Einstein's general theory of relativity and measuring continental drift.*

—**Professor Ingvar Lindgren**
Chairman of the Nobel Committee for Physics

As depicted by modern physics, atoms and their constituent "particles" are complex bundles of standing waves—flowerlike patterns of reverberating fields. Physicists who investigate matter at the level of these mystifying entities divide into two camps. The glamorous high-energy physicists smack particles together at enormous speed, comparable to the childlike strategy of selecting a hammer to investigate the innards of a clock. The gentler low-energy physicists tickle the vibrant little objects with nondestructive radiation and listen for a response.

The 1989 Nobel Prize in Physics went to three practitioners of the low-energy art, all of them tinkerers from childhood whose experimental contrivances have found applications not only in the world of pure science but in the world of practical affairs. Half the award went to Harvard University's Norman F. Ramsey, seventy-four, whose manifold contributions include masers, atomic clocks, and new ways to probe subatomic matter.

The other half of the prize was shared by two sometime colleagues, Hans G. Dehmelt, sixty-seven, of the University of Washington, and Wolfgang Paul, seventy-six, of the University of Bonn in West Germany. They are noted for inventing ways to herd, capture, and bottle particles, including devices that can hold a single particle suspended in majestic isolation for leisurely investigation over months at a time.

Sometimes collaboratively, sometimes competitively, the three laureates have pursued improvements in measurement precision necessary to uncover subtle effects that may have enormous implications for competing theories at both subatomic and cosmic levels. Taken together, their bottles and clocks have helped spawn new "single-particle physics," which is enriching the literature with profound insights about such things as the size and possible composite structure of the various inhabitants of the particle bestiary, about antimatter, about the origins and expansion of the universe, and about such abiding conundrums as whether the fundamental constants of nature are, in fact, all that constant.

Ramsey is now largely retired, except for guest lectureships and prestigious appointments (in 1989 he headed the committee that chilled the excitement about prospects for cold nuclear fusion). He still keeps an office at Harvard and continues to do research. The son of an army officer, he was born in Washington, D.C., and raised at various posts around the United States. Like most experimentalists, he was an ardent tinkerer in youth and almost became an engineer: "I didn't even know that there was such a thing as physics as a profession."

Happily enlightened on that score, he wound up studying physics at Columbia University, where he came under the influence of I. I. Rabi, one of the luminaries of atomic physics in the thirties and forties. At that time, Rabi was exploring implications of a suggestion made by Albert Einstein in 1915, namely that atoms could be stimulated to emit electromagnetic radiation by subject-

*N*orman Ramsey holds a "separated oscillatory field molecular beam apparatus."

ing them to radiation of the same frequency. According to then-evolving notions, atoms possess only discrete levels of energy. In the old-fashioned, solar-system model of the atom—billiard-ball electrons orbiting a billiard-ball nucleus—the energy levels corresponded to the heights of orbits. An electron got kicked to a higher orbit by absorbing electromagnetic radiation in the form of light or radio waves.

Even then, however, a fundamental quantum paradox was emerging that was to dismantle the billiard-ball, solar-system model. Einstein and others had shown that while light is wavelike, with higher frequency corresponding to higher energy content, it always comes in discrete packets, the way bullets emerge from a machine gun, not as a continuous stream the way water comes from a hose. Baffling as this dual wave-particle concept of light was—and for that matter still is—it had enormous impact. Taking their cue from light, physicists guessed that electrons and other particles might also have both wave- and particlelike properties. By now, thousands of experiments have proved them right. All particles behave sometimes like buckshot, hitting other particles, bouncing off them, and leaving visible tracks like jet trails in cloud or bubble chambers. But sometimes they behave like diffuse waves of water or sound: a single electron is somehow able to pass through two widely separated holes in a barrier simultaneously, like an ocean wave through two holes in a dike. Subsequently, the wave-segments somehow reemerge to produce a single bulletlike impact on a target. Recent experiments show that atoms behave much the same.

Mind-boggling as this was and is, it provided opportunities for applying powerful mathematical tools first developed to describe such complex events as wave vibrations and resonance. Before an electron shifts from one energy level to a higher one, it absorbs a quantum, or "photon," whose frequency characterizes that transition. Like all physical systems, atoms "prefer" lower energy levels: after an electron is pumped to some higher level, it eventually and randomly comes tumbling back to the lowest level, emitting a characteristic photon with each downward transition.

Einstein had concluded that electrons in higher-energy states could be stimulated to

*Ramsey, Dehmelt and Paul receive the Nobel Prize in Physics from His Majesty the King.*

*H.R.H. Princess Lillian of Sweden and Professor Ramsey at the Nobel Banquet.*

resonate up and down between two energy levels simply by illuminating them with light or other electromagnetic radiation of the proper frequency. These electrons would alternately absorb and emit photons of that frequency.

Whether they use high energies or low, physicists exploit the capacity for resonance (since found in all particles) to extract most of what they know. Rabi's low-energy "magnetic resonance" system and its various descendants have pinned down many properties of atoms, molecules, and their constituents. Invented in 1938, before lasers and other sources of pure high-frequency electromagnetic radiation, Rabi's device probed a peculiar very-low-energy gap—the "hyperfine transition" between two substates in the lowest energy state of the simplest atom of all, atomic hydrogen, which consists of a single electron orbiting a single proton.

This tiny energy gap exists because the proton, like many other particles, appears to be spinning, always at a constant rate of speed. Because of the proton's spin and positive electric charge, it behaves something like a little electromagnet, the exterior surface of which is coated with electric charge. As it spins, the rotating charge resembles the flow of electric current around the coil of wire of an electromagnet. Hence, the proton tends to align its axis of spin with the surrounding magnetic field just the way an electromagnet or compass needle would. Physicists call this tendency "magnetic moment."

To make the hydrogen atom take the first step up the energy ladder, flipping to the higher-energy "parallel" state, one subjects it to electromagnetic oscillations (i.e., radio waves) with a frequency of 1420 megahertz (MHz). This particular frequency corresponds to that with which the proton's spin axis tends to wobble around, or "precess," in a magnetic field, much the way a slowing gyroscope wobbles as it starts to fall from its orientation perpendicular to earth's gravitational field. After a brief but random period of exposure to this radiation, the proton will flip to the higher-energy parallel state; after another brief period it will flip back again, reemitting the 1420 MHz energy it absorbed in the first place.

In Rabi's magnetic resonance system, a beam of atoms, molecules, or other particles streams through a long evacuated chamber. The beam is so tenuous that the distance between particles averages something like a thousandth of a centimeter—an astronomical distance by atomic standards—so that the particles exert only small effects upon each another. The beam passes through a region containing two superimposed magnetic fields. One is a steady field to align the spin axes; the other is an oscillating field whose frequency experimenters can adjust until the rate is found at which spin axes are flipping to the parallel state at the maximum rate.

Magnetic resonance probing has now been extended to objects other than atomic beams, including neutron beams and liquids and solids. Since a particle's tendency to wobble and flip reflects a combination of circumstances, such as its charge, rate of spin, size, shape, and distribution of possible internal parts, magnetic resonance has

proved an enormously powerful diagnostic tool. Magnetic resonance imaging replaces X rays in many applications, providing graphic, colored, highly detailed images of, for example, internal organs of the human body.

Many such applications only became practical with Ramsey's improvements, which are mentioned in his Nobel citation. One trouble with Rabi's atomic beam device was that the long homogeneous magnetic field through which the beam passed was never all that homogeneous. As a result, before they emerged, many of the resonating atoms fell out of tune and phase, muddying interpretation of the experiment. In 1949 Ramsey replaced the single large oscillating field with two short oscillating regions, one before and one after the long homogeneous field region. Both oscillating fields were driven at the same frequency and phase; the first begins the flipping process; the second acts as a kind of filter to detect and pass only those atoms that maintain precisely a 1420 MHz frequency and phase after a considerable passage of time.

Variations on Ramsey's "separated oscillatory fields" principle are commonly found where exact knowledge of resonating particles is important. A well-known example is the cesium atomic clock adopted by international convention in 1967 as the world's standard timekeeper, replacing the standard based on the notoriously fickle rotation of the earth. A second of time is officially defined as 9,192,631,770 oscillations of the hyperfine transition in the cesium atom.

So, the rapid and exceedingly steady beat of the quantum atom has replaced slower oscillations of pendulums and quartz crystals as the beat to which humankind ultimately dances. Moreover, time is now the quantity that man can measure most precisely—so precisely, in fact, that most other common international standards are now based upon time in one way or another. The meter, or length standard, for instance, is defined in terms of the minuscule fraction of a second that light takes to travel a certain distance. And volume standards, such as the cubic centimeter, and weight standards, such as the gram, ultimately derive from the meter.

A cesium clock can in principle be built wherever anyone needs to know how long a second is. In fact, cesium clocks are bulky, touchy, expensive laboratory devices, hard to get running and hard to keep in tune. Nearly as accurate, but far more portable and stable, is another style of atomic clock based on the hydrogen maser, which Ramsey and Daniel Kleppner invented in 1960. The gas maser (an acronym for "microwave amplification of stimulated emission of radiation") is also grandfather to the laser, which operates at light rather than microwave frequencies.

Essentially, Ramsey's hydrogen maser modifies the beam magnetic resonance system by steering a beam of excited hydrogen atoms into a 15 cm teflon-lined metal cavity, exactly sized to resonate at the characteristic frequency of the hyperfine transition. There, the gas atoms bootstrap each other into oscillation, producing a microwave frequency precise enough to make the maser a practical alternative to the cumbersome cesium clock. While slightly less accurate, the hydrogen clock is smaller, lighter, and so

*Professor Dr. Wolfgang Paul and his wife, Doris Walch-Paul.*

stable that two hydrogen clocks would not vary from one another by as much as a second over hundreds of millions of years. Hydrogen maser clocks find wide use in radio astronomy, space missions, and the satellite-based navigation system used by ship captains and others needing exact knowledge of their position on the earth's surface.

To select, focus, and steer the atoms in his hydrogen maser and beam resonance systems, Ramsey relied on some of the particle-manipulating principles that are the specialty of his fellow Nobel laureate Wolfgang Paul. Born in 1913 in Lorenzkirch, now part of East Germany, Paul studied physics at the University of Göttingen. He was inducted into the German army at the beginning of World War II, before getting his doctoral degree. Near the end of the war, after serving for a period in an antiaircraft unit, Paul was released from the army to complete his thesis and to work on the problem of separating atomic isotopes.

Since then, Paul has specialized in manipulating atoms, molecules, and subatomic particles in a kind of particle jujitsu employing oscillating or intricately shaped fields to exploit the dynamics and handholds offered by these scintillating systems. His quadruple mass spectrometer, for instance, which was completed shortly after the war, relies on the fact that heavier atoms resist the pushing action of an oscillating electromagnetic field more than lighter ones do, separating the

two. It is now a standard device for separating and identifying components of unknown substances.

The six-pole focusing magnets used in gas masers rely on the opposite polarization of parallel and antiparallel atoms. Passing between the annular poles, the low-energy antiparallel particles are flipped aside while the excited parallel particles are focused and projected through a small hole into the resonant cavity. Ramsey also employed Paul's six-pole and four-pole devices to filter and focus the beam in his separated oscillating fields system.

Paul's electric bottle, known as the Paul trap, extends these principles to capture particles in a dead-end chamber and hold them there. Similar to the Paul trap is the Penning

*Professor Paul enjoys the company of Mrs. Ingrid Carlsson, wife of the Swedish Prime Minister.*

trap, invented by Paul's longtime friend and coworker Hans Dehmelt. (Dehmelt named it after a Dutch physicist who perfected a cylindrical ionizing device that worked on similar principles.) The main difference between the Paul and Penning traps is that the former uses oscillating fields to trap ions (atoms from which one or more electrons have been added or removed), while the latter employs interlocked electric and magnetic fields that do not oscillate.

Born in Görlitz, now East Germany, in 1922, Dehmelt was an experimentalist from childhood. Hans Geiger, inventor of the Geiger counter, was a tenant in his family's house, and Dehmelt took piano lessons from Geiger's daughter. Like Paul, he served in an antiaircraft unit. He fought in Russia, and later in the Battle of the Bulge, he was captured by the Americans. He spent a year in a prison camp, where he repaired Allied X-ray equipment and radios and even built a radio for French workers at the prison.

After the war, Dehmelt entered graduate school at Göttingen and eventually became a teaching assistant in the physics department at a time when Paul was also an assistant. Seven years older than Dehmelt, Paul had already designed some of his quadruple mass filters and focusing devices, inexpensive tools by comparison with the cyclotrons and other glamorous devices that the wealthy American universities had access to.

By that time, the great quantum theorists like Werner Heisenberg and Wolfgang Pauli had not only destroyed the classical billiard-ball image of particles but even seemed to have ruled out prospects that the elusive objects would ever hold still to allow experimentalists to measure them in the classical manner: the very act of measurement would forever alter the object being measured. Chalky-fingered theoreticians glory in such conundrums, but experimentalists like Paul and Dehmelt yearn for something more perceptible—something corresponding to the dot their Göttingen professor drew on the blackboard one day, saying, "This is an electron."

In 1952 Dehmelt entered Duke University as a post-doctoral student, later moving to the University of Washington as an assistant professor. He has remained at Washington ever since, except for occasional returns to Germany to work with Paul in trapping particles.

While the early traps built by Paul, Dehmelt, and others could bottle particles, they could not clamp them into the blackboard-dot stillness that Dehmelt craved. Instead, the particles entered the traps at considerable velocity and then circled or bounced around inside like frantic fish. To physicists, such particles are simply "hot," like molecules in a heated gas, the main difference being that in their high-vacuum surroundings, trapped particles have a vastly greater range of motion.

After developing his Penning trap in the early seventies, Dehmelt sought some way of chilling his trapped particles to stillness. The development of the dye laser, which is tunable over a range of frequencies, provided the means. To understand laser cooling, imagine that an ion is bouncing rapidly back and forth along a straight path inside a trap. A laser beam is directed along that path from one end. If the laser is tuned to the

*Hans Dehmelt holding the inside of his Penning trap. The painting in the background is a barium ion painted by his brother.*



right frequency, some of the ion's electrons will resonate between energy states, alternately absorbing light quanta from the beam, then reemitting quanta of the same frequency. To effect cooling, the laser is tuned to a frequency slightly below the electron's normal resonant frequency. That's because the Doppler effect of the ion's own movement appears to shift the laser's frequency, just as it shifts the apparent sound of a passing train whistle.

All the quanta absorbed from the beam come from a single direction, while the reemitted quanta emerge in random directions. So, the net effect is to slow the ion.

In 1979 Paul, Dehmelt, and several colleagues, working in Germany, trapped and cooled a single barium ion in a tiny Paul trap only 0.2 mm long. They playfully christened it Astrid and held it practically motionless for six hours while recording its behavior and even photographed it with an ordinary camera. At about the same time, an American team that included one of Dehmelt's former students, David Wineland, managed a similar feat with a mercury ion in a Penning trap. Since then, the members of the burgeoning new field of single-particle physics have trapped other ions, electrons, positrons (the electron's antiparticle), protons, antiprotons, and various combinations of the above.

Single-particle physics is attractive because it permits investigations on some of the most perfect experimental subjects in science—the protons, electrons, neutrons, and so forth that, inside a trap, hang isolated in a void relatively much vaster than the one that surrounds our solar system. Stroked by the bow of radio frequency or laser light, they ring with chords of pure cosmic tones, cleaner responses to elemental laws of nature than displayed in any other experiment man has devised.

The people who keep the world's time are already salivating at the prospect of clocks that tick at the rate of a single resonating atom but are ten thousand times more accurate than the clunky old cesium and hydrogen clocks they have now. Inaccuracies in present-day clocks arise from Doppler shifts due to movement of the atoms and from discordant tones as the atoms bang into each other or the material walls of their resonant chambers. Prototypes of superaccurate single-particle clocks have been investigated by Dehmelt, Wineland, and others. Dehmelt's version involves suspending a barium ion such as Astrid in a Paul trap and then exciting it with blue laser light until the electron in the proper energy state glows with the same visible shade of blue. "That's to establish communication with the ion," Dehmelt explains.

Simultaneously, the atom is illuminated with another laser beam that competes with the first beam. Its purpose is to stimulate the same electron to make a different downward transition, one far less probable than the first—so improbable that it only happens every thirty seconds on the average. According to the laws of quantum mechanics, to accomplish a transition that improbable requires an extremely precise frequency. The experimenters keep adjusting the second laser until the ion suddenly ceases to glow, indicating that the second type of transition has occurred. In a real atomic clock, that second frequency would become the new world time standard.

Physicists have more at stake in single-particle physics than making clocks and exhibiting trapping prowess, however. Many of the fundamental questions about the nature of matter and the universe hinge on measurements so difficult as to confound the ingenuity of earth-bound science. The true nature of the electron, for instance, is so enigmatic that Einstein was driven to observe, "You know, it would be sufficient to

*Hans Dehmelt examines his prize at the Nobel Foundation, beneath a portrait of Alfred Nobel.*

really understand the electron."

Currently, low-energy physicists spend much of their effort trying to refine and extend their greatest triumph—the theory of relativistic quantum electrodynamics, or QED, the mathematical description of the electromagnetic behavior of the atom that evolved in the first half of this century. QED stands as the most triumphant description of nature science has yet produced, experimentally proven to many decimal places, accounting for all chemistry and most solid-state phenomena. Nevertheless, QED contains some awkward assumptions, including the assumption that the electron is a dimensionless point.

Dimensionless particles present several paradoxes. Since the electron is known to possess electric charge, for instance, without size it would seem to require infinite energy to hold this ball of repellent electrical force together. And infinite energy, of course, translates to infinite mass. Theorists have managed to devise clever mathematics to skirt such problems in QED, but Dehmelt and his colleagues now seem to have found that the electron does indeed have a size.

One method of determining size and structure in spinning charged particles like protons and electrons is to measure what's called their "gyromagnetic ratio" or "g factor," a constant that relates a particle's magnetic moment to the momentum of its spin, or angular momentum. In a billiard-ball particle, angular momentum depends not only on the particle's mass and rate of spin but on size—how the mass is distributed outward from the center. So, knowing mass, spin, angular momentum, and g, one should, in principle, be able to determine size.

Paul Dirac, the English physicist who refined QED to make it consistent with relativity in the 1930s, predicted that the electron g factor would be precisely 2, a figure consistent with the electron having no size at all. While QED attained its enormous success despite that paradoxical assumption, a virtual industry of experimentalists has sought to measure g.

In 1984 Dehmelt and one of his former students, Robert van Dyck, trapped and cooled a single electron for many months inside a Penning trap. They named it Priscilla and, among other things, proceeded to try to measure Priscilla's g. Using finely tuned radio transmitters and receivers to perturb Priscilla and listen to her various electromagnetic whines as she spun and oscillated inside her cage, they arrived at a figure for g of 2.00000000110 rather than Dirac's simple 2, consistent with an electron radius of something less than $10-20$ cm.

Successful in both mathematical prediction and practical results, quantum science troubles even its practitioners with its philosophical and conceptual difficulties—its indeterminacies and apparent paradoxes. Perhaps the leisurely, closely controlled contemplation of isolated particles may bring some resolution. Dehmelt believes that some of the accepted wisdom about the quantum world—that attempts to measure properties of a given particle must irrevocably alter those properties, for instance—are overstated at best. Astrid, Priscilla, and their ilk allowed people to go on repeating measurements to their heart's desire.

Many other long-standing questions—about prospects of mass in the ubiquitous but long-presumed-massless neutrino; about whether antimatter falls up in a gravitational field rather than down; about the origins of a preferential "left-handedness," or parity-violation, in certain particle behaviors; about whether various physical constants such as gravitational force are slowly changing as the universe expands, to name only a few—now seem experimentally addressable because of the clocks and bottles that the newest Nobel laureates in Physics helped develop.

The Nobel Prize laureates Altman and Cech.

# CHAPTER 4

# THE NOBEL PRIZE IN CHEMISTRY

## THE WORK OF PROFESSOR SIDNEY ALTMAN AND PROFESSOR THOMAS R. CECH

*The discovery of catalytic RNA came as a great surprise and was indeed met with a certain amount of skepticism. Who could ever have suspected that scientists, as recently as in our own decade, were missing such a fundamental component in their understanding of the molecular prerequisites of life? Altman's and Cech's discoveries not only mean that the introductory chapters of our chemistry and biology textbooks will have to be rewritten, they also herald a new way of thinking and are a call to new biochemical research.*

**—Professor Bertil Andersson**
Member of the Nobel Committee for Chemistry

Among biochemists, there is a gentleman's agreement about how to treat seemingly outlandish ideas that appear in one's in-box: Either categorize them as crackpot, or consider the remote possibility that they may some day be worthy of mention when the Nobel Committee at the Royal Swedish Academy of Sciences comes around for nominations. The trouble is, it is not always easy to recognize the difference.

Take Sidney Altman, professor of biology (and recently retired dean) at Yale University, for example. He recalls the dark days of 1977 when he tried to publish a paper describing new findings about the ribonucleic acid (RNA) molecule. That paper was "rejected out of hand with hardly any review. I think the referees thought it was too outlandish, but I didn't take offense. They just had no idea what we were talking about."

Today, however, biologists ranging from the high school student dissecting frogs to the Nobel Committee in Sweden know what Altman was talking about. He and biochemist Thomas Cech of the University of Colorado at Boulder independently stumbled upon an outlandish side of nature, and in so doing, they toppled a decades-old dogma. They found that RNA, which was previously thought to function merely as a carrier of genetic information (much as blueprints carry architectural information), can propel chemical reactions inside a living cell. RNA, they said, can function as a catalyst. It was like discovering that blueprints can assemble themselves into a gabled gingerbread Victorian mansion without any help from hammers and saws.

For about as long as biologists had understood the genetic machinery of the cell, their central dogma held that the biomolecules inside living cells had a division of labor as fine as anything Henry Ford had invented. As the master molecule of heredity, deoxyribonucleic acid (DNA) holds all the genetic information of the organism. All animals and plants contain copies of this information in each cell. The DNA is copied into RNA, its sister molecule, which translates the genetic code and conveys the information to the cell's protein factories, called ribosomes. There, the RNA directs the production of proteins—everything from the enzymes that power biochemical reactions to the very blood, muscle, and other tissues that constitute the creature. Proteins and nucleic acids, then, are the two critical ingredients of life.

In the 1970s Altman and Cech (pronounced "check") were investigating two unrelated puzzles, neither of which seemed to have anything to do with RNA catalysis. They were studying how DNA is copied into RNA and how RNA directs the production of proteins. DNA strands are not straightfor-

ward manufacturing instructions; rather, they often contain long lengths of nonsense, as two researchers found in 1977. This gob-

*Professors Altman and Cech receive the Prize in Chemistry.*

bledygook codes for nothing; nonetheless, it is also copied into RNA. That means that the cell must take drastic action to keep the nonsense from reaching the so-called protein factory. The solution: snip out the nonsense en route to the ribosome and rejoin the ends of the RNA so that it once again makes a coherent, useful molecule. This snipping and splicing requires enzymes, biological catalysts so important that, as the Nobel committee said in honoring the pair, "without enzymes there would be no life." While searching for these editing enzymes, Cech discovered that the job is done not by a roving journeyman molecule but by the RNA itself.

The find did not go over well in the biochemical fraternity. Before this discovery, scientists were convinced that neither nucleic acids nor enzymes could exist without the other. DNA needs enzymes to copy it into RNA and make proteins. But proteins need DNA to provide the instructions for their assembly. Since these are the two building blocks of life—the molecules that differentiate us from, say, rocks—this interdependence had been an insurmountable obstacle to explaining how the first living molecules emerged from the abiotic soup. (The biochemist's version of the chicken-and-egg question goes like this: Which came first, the nucleic acid or the protein?) The work of Cech and Altman goes a long way to resolving the mystery.

Cech was born in Chicago on December 8, 1947, and credits his father, a physician, with sparking his interest in science. "Anything he comes across, he wants to dissect, analyze, and understand at the level of

## PROFESSOR SIDNEY ALTMAN ACCEPTANCE REMARKS (excerpt)

In an era when being on the "cutting edge" of one's field is given so much weight, our colleagues may have wondered at times whether the edge we were on was perhaps the "back edge." One of us was working with a strange organism (*Tetrahymena thermophila*), the other with a familiar organism (*Escherichia coli*) but with a strange enzyme that somehow needed to carry around an RNA molecule to do its job. Furthermore, neither of our research groups set out in search of RNA catalysis. Thomas Cech and his group initially attributed the activity of their *Tetrahymena* RNA to a protein contaminant, and they only slowly succumbed to the weight of the accumulated data that argued for the RNA. My group established that Ribonuclease P contained an RNA as well as a protein component, and initially there was no reason to suspect that the RNA was responsible for the catalytic activity. Thus, the pathways leading to the discoveries of RNA catalysis were not as direct as one might imagine from reading about the results in textbooks. We are very fortunate to be recognized here in such an extraordinary manner for work that we enjoy.

physics," Cech says. He loved science fairs and threw himself with abandon into childhood science projects, focusing on rock collecting and fossils. He was "studious to the point of boring," he says, and his determination was paired with an unquenchable curiosity: when his family moved to Iowa, the teenage Cech would knock at the offices of geologists at the local university, ask questions, and examine their specimens for hours.

In college, Cech decided to leave behind rocks and fossils and concentrate on chemistry. But when he and his wife, Carol, also a chemist, spent a summer at the Lawrence Radiation Laboratory in Berkeley, California, Cech remembers, he was dismayed by the prospect of spending "several years doing

### PROFESSOR LARS GYLLENSTEN
### CHAIRMAN OF THE BOARD OF THE NOBEL FOUNDATION
### OPENING ADDRESS (excerpt)

Thirty years ago, Sir C. P. (later Lord) Snow excited great attention with his book *The Two Cultures and the Scientific Revolution*. Its basic thesis was that there is a dichotomy between, on the one hand, the humanities, on the other, our scientific and technological culture. One difference, according to Snow, was that the humanistic culture laid claim to a greater prestige. In the public mind, the word "culture" was taken to mean art, music, literature and the theater, history, philosophy and other humanistic disciplines. The natural sciences and technology, on the other hand, were *terra incognita* to most people. They were matter for the specialized journals to which the general public had no access, and in which it had no interest. From the financial aspect, however, science and technology was the richer of these two ill-matched brothers. Poverty per se was also seen as a particular virtue on the part of the poorer brother. How noble it was to base one's *oeuvre* on something other than

money and the good things in life. Snow's book excited great attention, but it was also, in parts, heavily criticized. On the whole, however, the truth of his thesis was conceded: he had pointed to anomalies that few felt able to deny.

This year the Royal Swedish Academy of Sciences celebrates its 250th anniversary. Its jubilee celebrations included a symposium on the history of science, called "Solomon's House Revisited." The title refers to Francis Bacon's Utopia, as envisaged in the early 17th century, in which Solomon's House is a great scientific institution within which science and technology create Utopia's riches and well-being—and promise more of the same for the future.

Francis Bacon is one of the founding fathers of modern scientific optimism. Our western culture has long been stamped with his view of the benefits and opportunities offered by organized science. Since Snow's day, the roles appear to have been reversed. Science and technology have wrested to themselves the supreme authority in our modern society. One of Bacon's most famous dicta is that knowledge is power. And "knowledge" has come to be equated increasingly with scientific knowledge.

In recent years, however, a new swing of the pendulum can be discerned. We have become aware of the damage and the hazards that have arisen from uncritical economic expansion, consequences that were unforeseen. Just now, the focus is directed above all upon damage in the ozone layer, and the increase in the carbon dioxide content of the atmosphere. The felling of the rain forests and other encroachments on the environment are killing off whole vegetable and animal species. It is impoverishing the future genetic resources of our life sphere—and constitutes a morally indefensible assault upon other living creatures.

The proposition that knowledge is power has become a dubious one. All use of power is not beneficial. And it often seems as if the "power" of knowledge is utterly impotent. The development of our societies is steered by forces other than foresight, responsibility and wise stewardship. A research worker in today's world recalls the prophetess Cassandra, who knew what the future bore in its womb but was unable to prevent it. When her prophecies were inconvenient, they were disbelieved.

Increasing demands are now being raised to bring the two cultures together. Researchers and technologists are seeking contact with humanists and social scientists. Similar demands are being made from the humanistic world for a well-considered view of how technology and science should be used in the service of humanity, and for what has been termed "sustainable life." The steadily increasing demand for responsibility on the part of both the researchers and the humanists is now bridging the gap between the two cultures.

The matter of protecting our environment and our resources so that we can all live a decent and dignified life in the future is not a task for specialists. It is the concern of everyone, and it is a global problem. These aims are incompatible with the shortsighted economic and political programs that now steer our industrial societies. The task of the researchers is to create and spread knowledge, and to develop ways to render unpopular measures politically feasible. This presents a challenge: How can a democratic society introduce measures that will strike at our present living habits in the short term but are necessary for humanity's standard of life in the long term?

In Alfred Nobel's own program for the Nobel Prize it is possible to discern an effort to combine science and technology with humanitarian ideals and international solidarity.

a lot of what I call sophisticated plumbing—putting together a complex apparatus and making sure you get almost every last gas molecule pumped out of it in preparation for doing an experiment."

Then he met DNA. As a graduate student at the University of California at Berkeley, in the early 1970s Cech met chemists who were engaged in the furthest imaginable thing from plumbing. They were "bouncing off the walls with excitement about chromosomes and DNA, something that I knew almost nothing about," Cech says. He decided to sign on and study the chemistry of living cells. (Carol was also hooked: she now specializes in the control of gene expression in the bacterium *Escherichia coli*.) "I think of myself as being extremely fortunate to be spending my time in something that I'm so

head-over-heels excited about," says Cech.

The joy is in the work itself, not the results, Cech believes. "It would be a mistake for anyone to go into the science as a means to an end, because it's the process that's the exciting part." As often as not, the difference between Nobel-winning work and less-lauded research is serendipity. "You have to have been lucky enough that the thing that you were working on turned out to be of incredible importance to a big sector of science as a whole," Cech explains.

Cech and his colleagues were indeed lucky enough, or insightful enough, to happen upon a profoundly interesting and important puzzle. The work began in 1978, when Cech decided to tackle the puzzle of how RNA containing nonsense code edited out the junk so that it was a strand of pure, useful genetic information. He chose to ask the question of a single-celled ciliated protozoan named *Tetrahymena thermophila*. Its virtue was that its genes work just like those of higher organisms (including humans), but they can be grown by the bucketful very easily. In addition, each *Tetrahymena* contains ten thousand copies of a particular gene, rather than the one or two in a human cell, and thus yields much more of the material to study.

Like genes of higher organisms, those of *Tetrahymena* contain nonsense segments. These noncoding stretches are called introns. They, like the rest of the DNA, are copied into RNA. But before the RNA can transport meaningful instructions to the cell's protein-making machinery (the ribosome organelle), the RNA has to splice out the nonsense. Conventional wisdom held

*Sidney Altman and Ann Körner, his wife.*

*T*homas Cech, his wife, Dr. Carol Cech, and their daughter Allison.

that an enzyme acted as the scissors and paste, snipping out the intron and rejoining the sheared ends. Without enzymes, the cell would take seventeen thousand years to half-finish the job; a catalyst makes the splicing proceed in less than a minute. Cech and company decided to purify and identify the cellular machinery responsible for the splicing.

"There was really only one candidate for the machinery," says Cech. "It would be a group of protein enzymes. There was no question about that." Cech managed to purify unspliced RNA. He incubated it with a stew of chemicals found in the *Tetrahymena* cell nucleus, where splicing occurs naturally.

"We assumed [the extracts] would serve as a source of the putative splicing enzymes," Cech recalls. Indeed, "the splicing occurred right away" in the cell extracts. So far, so good. Then the impossible happened. As a control experiment, Cech's team marinated the unspliced RNA in a solution with no extracts from the cell nucleus. The RNA spliced anyway. "This wasn't one of the possible outcomes of the experiment," Cech notes dryly.

The chemical machinery was presumed to be in the soup that constituted the cell nucleus. How could RNA be spliced in the absence of these enzymes? Cech asked his technician, Art Zogg, to repeat the experi-

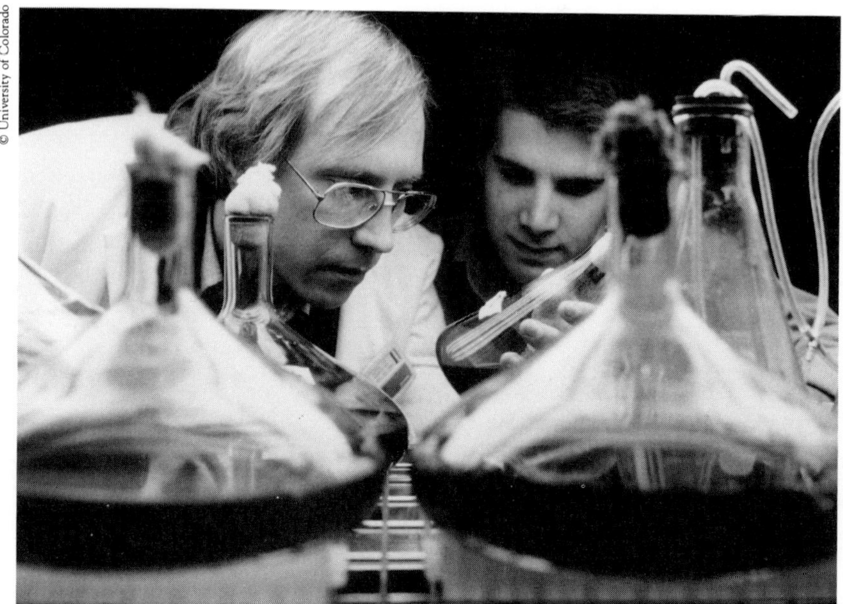



*Thomas Cech in his classroom at the University of Colorado at Boulder.*

ment, since something must be wrong. Zogg repeated it five times during the next few weeks, getting the same result each time. "The RNA seemed to be able to cut and rejoin itself," says Cech. But that wasn't what they concluded at the time because "that wasn't on the list of allowable interpretations," he emphasizes. Rather, Cech worried that perhaps the intron he saw being expelled had really been spliced before and was simply caught up in the tangled skein of RNA. It might have been that "all we were watching in our test tube was some kind of untangling reaction," Cech explains.

To determine whether true splicing was occurring required more sophisticated chemistry and a year off to develop the proper techniques. "I decided to do a totally crazy experiment," Cech says. "I was very busy teaching at the time. I had the RNA in the freezer waiting. I just needed to find a few hours of peace and quiet to do the experiment. And I had a feeling that the result was also sort of sitting in there waiting, calling to me, and all I had to do was find the time to let it tell me what the answer was going to be."

No one ever said academic science was easy. Cech's teaching and research schedule leaves him little time for what would otherwise be favorite activities, such as playing with his two children and cooking. Even skiing, which Cech discovered when he moved to Colorado, is a rare pleasure, but he finds that racing down the slopes lets him "completely forget about the petty problems of what's going on in the laboratory or the latest grant proposal."

Yet, once he finally stole the time to listen to that muse in his freezer, Cech performed

46

what would turn out to be the pivotal experiment. He had seen clues that guanosine (the G in GTP, a small molecule that seemed necessary for the splicing reaction) was bonding to the intron. To prove this, Cech mixed unspliced RNA with radioactively labeled GTP. "It worked the first time," Cech still marvels: the RNA became radioactively labeled, indicating the G had bonded. "I ran from the laboratory back to my office and sketched out the mechanism of what must be happening. It took only a few minutes."

In 1981 Cech published his explanation for the splicing reaction. He thought that the intron, or nonsense part of RNA, binds the guanosine and moves it in such a way as to sever the chemical bond between the sense and nonsense sequences. After a series of self-catalyzed reactions, a loop of nonsense RNA splices itself out and rejoins its ends. The intact RNA, freed of its nonsense, proceeds to the protein-making factory.

There was a slight possibility that rogue protein had managed to latch onto the RNA and was catalyzing the reaction. "We treated the RNA in all kinds of dastardly ways [to remove any protein catalysts]." They boiled it in detergent and added enzymes that chew up proteins. Nothing changed—the RNA was still spliced. But the seemingly inescapable conclusion that there was no protein there after all was counter to everything they knew, and so the Colorado team could not believe their own lab results. "We kept having doubts and had to spend a lot of time convincing ourselves," Cech recalls. After more experiments in 1981 and 1982 to rule out the possibility, the conclusion was inescapable: RNA was self-splicing. It was a cat-

alyst. The scientific crew had a champagne party and sat around thinking of clever names for the versatile RNA. The winner: ribozyme.

Yet their colleagues didn't exactly shower them with hosannas. "Many people in the scientific community thought this was a curiosity." Cech recalls. Altman didn't even receive the courtesy. Even before Cech's group had met their first *Tetrahymena*, Altman had begun working with *Escherichia coli*, the ubiquitous human-gut bacterium. In 1978 he was studying an enzyme that cut *E. coli*'s RNA. This molecular scissors, named ribonuclease-P (RNase-P), consists of one protein and one RNA molecule. When Altman's student Ben Stark split this enzyme and separated the protein, the dissection crippled the enzyme. Its activity was restored only when the two components were remixed. Apparently, both protein and nucleic acid were essential for making RNase-P work.

Altman remembers encountering "resistance and bitterness, which in some cases one could almost term hostility," he says of the reaction to this early work, which was finally published in 1976. "But I felt that the truth wins out in the end, and in this case it certainly did." Altman and Stark's experiment was the first to show that RNA is necessary for an enzyme to work.

Altman, born and raised in Montreal, wanted to study physics in college. "Scientists and science figured prominently in the end of the Second World War, and as a young boy that certainly impressed me," Altman explains. No one in his family had attended college, and few had even finished

*Sidney Altman performs an experiment in a Yale University laboratory.*



high school (his father owned a small grocery store). Yet, when Altman was twelve, a family member gave him a book about the periodic table of elements. "I remember it vividly," he says. "It impressed me with the beauty of the scientific theory."

Two years after Cech discovered that RNA could splice itself, Altman's team found that RNA alone, without the protein everyone believed to be the real enzymatic workhorse, could cut certain precursors to RNA. This was the second example of RNA catalysis but the first true example of an enzyme, in that the RNA was acting on something other than itself. By comparison, RNA catalysts are today so common that discovery of yet another may be published.

Cech explains, "but not in the very best journals."

Still, scientists are only beginning to realize the importance of RNA catalysts. First and foremost, the discovery upsets biology's central dogma and thus "enables us to think in a deeper way and in a more precise way about the processes of life," Cech says. Altman adds, "While our first purpose is simply to discover things about nature that were not known before, all of us hope that what we do will in some way benefit mankind."

One of those benefits might be esoteric but no less satisfying: a clue to the origin of life itself. If RNA can "do something other than just sit there and be a passive carrier of genetic information, this . . . would allow us to understand how life began," explains Altman. The difficulty previously had been the interdependence of DNA and proteins, both of which are so crucial to life that they can be considered the chemicals that define it. DNA requires proteins in order to function. But proteins are produced by DNA. So what emerged from the primordial soup first?

Neither DNA nor proteins can apparently exist, let alone emerge, without the other. RNA catalysis may provide a way out. "You can well imagine how the first primitive biochemical systems might have been composed almost solely of RNA," explains Altman. "Imagine that RNA molecules replicated themselves and carried out various other functions needed to preserve these systems and enable them to reproduce."

Another, more practical spin-off of the discovery of RNA catalysis might involve fighting viruses. Many viruses that attack humans—from the common cold and polio to hepatitis and AIDS—have their genes in the form of RNA, rather than DNA as humans do. It might be possible one day to use RNA enzymes to cut up particular RNAs that are infecting cells.

Much remains to be done, both in terms of the basic science involved—the search of RNA catalysis—and the possible applications. One remaining challenge, for example, involves locating the "active site" on the RNA strand to which the catalyst attaches itself (a search much like looking for a keyhole in the dark).

At least biologists know where *not* to file the latest missives about this astonishing aspect of the chemistry of life: under "Crackpot."

*The laureates in Physics and Chemistry at the Royal Academy of Sciences. (Left to right) Cech, Dehmelt, Ramsey, Paul, Altman.*

On the evening of December 10, the Nobel banquet is held in the Blue Hall of Stockholm's City Hall (right). The center table is reserved for honored guests, including (from left) Prince Bertil, Ellie Ramsey, wife of Physics laureate Norman Ramsey, and King Carl Gustaf. Baron Stig Ramel (top), President of the Nobel Foundation, enjoys the banquet entertainment, as laureate Thomas Cech dances with his young daughter (above).

# THE NOBEL BANQUET

*The Nobel Prize laureates Bishop and Varmus.*

# CHAPTER 5

# THE NOBEL PRIZE IN PHYSIOLOGY OR MEDICINE

## THE WORK OF PROFESSOR J. MICHAEL BISHOP AND PROFESSOR HAROLD E. VARMUS

*To their own great surprise and that of the scientific community, Bishop and Varmus concluded that the tumor-inducing gene in the Rous virus was of cellular origin. Does this mean we are carrying cancer genes in our cells? Obviously not. However, in our cells there is a family of probably several hundred genes which are old in evolutionary terms and which control the normal growth and division of cells. Disruptions in the functioning of one or more of these genes can cause one cell to slip out of the network of growth controls. The cell runs amok and a tumor may be the result.*

**—Professor Erling Norrby**
Deputy Chairman of the Nobel Assembly, Karolinska Institute

When you talk to J. Michael Bishop and Harold Varmus, the University of California-San Francisco scientists who won the 1989 Nobel Prize in Medicine or Physiology, the conversation automatically starts with the subject of cancer. After all, their pioneering research in 1976 overturned contemporary thinking about cancer's origins and set research off on a new and now dominant direction. Bishop and Varmus were the first to establish clearly that we all carry the potential for cancer in our normal hereditary makeup and that solving the mystery of the dread disease lies in understanding the normal cell and why it sometimes goes awry. That seems a simple insight, but a critical one. As Bishop puts it, "I don't think there's

*The laureates receive the Nobel Prize in Physiology or Medicine from His Majesty the King.*

any doubt that the work we did and the work that grew out of it has given us a view of the cancer cell that's detailed and promising beyond all reasonable hope of ten years ago."

Yet, after a few more minutes spent with either man, in their laboratories high on Parnassus Avenue above the Golden Gate, talk quickly veers off into other, unexpected and illuminating directions. Although Bishop, a slight, bearded, reflective fifty-three-year-old with a self-deprecating sense of humor, and Varmus, tall and quick-talking, would be embarrassed to be considered Renaissance men, their range of interests and command of knowledge beyond mere science is impressive, not to say startling. A chat with Varmus glides smoothly from a discussion of today's *New York Times* op-ed page to the prose of Umberto Eco, to the pleasures of bicycling in the early morning San Francisco fog. Bishop talks knowledgeably about Confederate tactics at Gettysburg, the literary quality of the Old Testament, or the place of baseball in American life.

Bishop displayed his eclecticism on the day the Nobel awards were announced. To the bemusement of the media, he insisted that the UCSF press conference concerning the prize be scheduled for 8:30 A.M. so he could attend the San Francisco Giants–Chicago Cubs National League playoff game that day. After all, he said, he had been a baseball fan since he was five years old, and he wasn't going to miss San Francisco's bid for its first World Series appearance in twenty-five years merely because of a Nobel Prize. The newspaper stories made him sound like your average rabid bleacherite, lost in the arcane statistics of runs batted in and number of times caught stealing, but his approach to baseball is more philosophical. Like the late Bartlett Giamatti, the Renaissance scholar and Yale president who became baseball commissioner, he sees baseball as a mirror of life—joys and sorrows and hard-learned lessons. Bishop spent his boyhood lying in front of an old RCA console radio, following the broadcast fortunes and misfortunes of the hapless Philadelphia Athletics of the 1940s. "You couldn't get any lower than the Athletics in those days," he says with a rueful smile, "so I learned to suffer at an early age and to deal with disappointment. As Bart Giamatti said, the game is designed to break your heart."

This same philosophical eloquence was evident in his Nobel Lecture. Bishop told the Stockholm audience:

"I have learned that there is no single path to creativity, not even within the stern halls of science. . . . We are constrained not by the necessary discipline of rigor, but by the limits to our imaginations and our intellectual courage.

"Discovery takes two forms. The first is mundane, but nevertheless legitimate: we grope our way to reality and then recognize it for what it is. The second is legitimate, but also sublime: we imagine reality as it ought to be and then find the proof for our imaginings.

"I have been fortunate to know the first form of discovery and am thankful for the privilege. I have miscarried opportunities to know the second and am diminished by the failure. Redemption lies in more imaginings."

*J. Michael Bishop at the Karolinska Institute.*

That these two men should range so far beyond the specialized world of molecular biology should not be surprising. Neither started out with ambitions to be a researcher—nor even a scientist. Bishop, the son of a rural Pennsylvania clergyman, attended a two-room school where "science lessons consisted of gathering and pressing wildflowers." At Gettysburg College, a small liberal-arts institution not far from home, he took "the mandatory major" in chemistry but gorged himself with courses in history, art, philosophy, and literature. "I've never been happier than when I was in college—I was like a kid in a candy shop," he says. When he entered Harvard Medical School, it was with the vague notion of continuing in academic life as a teacher of medicine. "Then I discovered that the entryway to an academic career was through this enterprise called research, which I hadn't heard of at Gettysburg. And the rest, as they say in sportspeak, is history."

*Varmus and Bishop pose with a portrait of Alfred Nobel.*

Varmus, whose father was a doctor in suburban Freeport, New York, assumed he would follow in the paternal footsteps. He became enamored of journalism at Amherst College, however, and then sidestepped medical school to accept a Woodrow Wilson Fellowship and pursue a graduate degree in literature at Harvard. "But," he says, "that year I found myself feeling dissatisfied; I felt I was slipping into the soft sands of academic scholarship in a way that was going to make me feel detached from the real world. I started going to Harvard Medical School on Saturday mornings to look in on clinical pathology conferences, and envied my friends who were participatory rather than merely spectators. So I applied again to med-

ical school, and this time I took it."

The two arrived at UCSF by similarly circuitous routes. Bishop's sudden infatuation with research led him to persuade Harvard to let him forswear the traditional fourth-year medical school curriculum in favor of a year in the laboratory. He whizzed through a Massachusetts General Hospital internship, with no intention of ever practicing clinical medicine, and then went to the National Institutes of Health (NIH) for two years, under a program for young scholars. He spent a year in Hamburg, Germany, completing a project with an NIH colleague, and then looked about for a medical-school appointment. "A prestigious place on the East Coast" offered him a position. But "the prestigious place did not need me. This place, UCSF, looked like it needed me. So I came here."

Varmus followed Bishop to NIH and then went west as his appointment was ending. "For a variety of reasons having to do with fishing and a love of the outdoors and a need to be in a new environment, I was very interested in coming to California, so I came out here and went shopping," he recalls. Bishop, a lowly assistant professor who had arrived only the year before ("I was still the new kid on the block"), interviewed him. Both are vague on the details of that first meeting (Bishop remembers that Varmus wore a beard; Varmus denies it), but they soon recognized that their interests overlapped and their abilities were complementary, so Varmus signed on as a postdoctoral fellow in Bishop's lab.

Those were the heady days of President Nixon's "war on cancer," when the government believed that throwing large amounts of research money at the disease would unlock its secrets and lead to a cure. One of the primary areas of research was the possibility of a viral explanation for the disease. Viruses had been discovered in various cancer cells and some researchers believed that some virus (or viruses) was the cause of all cancers. A particular suspect was a large and mysterious family of viruses now known as retroviruses. These viruses were found in the ribonucleic acid (RNA) of animal cells and were known to cause cancer in these animals. The great unknown was how the viruses managed to replicate themselves and thus cause tumors. Bishop had studied viruses at NIH; Varmus had worked with ap-

propriate assaying techniques. The two took aim at a possible research project into retrovirus replication, and Varmus went back east to finish up his work and collect his belongings.

By the time he returned, two bits of important research had changed the playing field. Howard Temin and David Baltimore (who would be named Nobel laureates in 1975) had identified an enzyme, called reverse transcriptase, which allowed the virus to move backward from the RNA of the cell, which carries out the genetic instructions, and invade the deoxyribonucleic acid (DNA), which contains the genetic program. Thus, it could encode its own replication in the cell's genes. This, of course, was the direction opposite the usual DNA-RNA route. Temin had been suggesting this backward route since the early 1960s, but the idea had not been accepted until the discovery of reverse transcriptase.

Meanwhile, at the University of California, Steven Martin and his colleagues isolated a mutant of the Rous sarcoma virus, a virus known to cause cancer in chickens, and found that it contained one clearly definable gene that enabled the virus to cause cancer but was independent of the functions required for growth.

About the same time, two NIH scientists offered an explanation for the virus-cancer link. Robert Huebner and George Todaro suggested that viruses had become incorporated into human cells eons ago and their genes had been passed down through the generations and were in the germ line for good. According to this theory, all cancer had a common retroviral origin. But the viral gene lay dormant until turned on by a mutation or by a carcinogen, or cancer-causing substance. Huebner and Todaro called these errant genes "oncogenes," or tumor genes.

Varmus and Bishop decided to test the oncogene theory by using the Rous sarcoma virus as a prototype. This fairly well understood cancer-causing virus had been identified long before by Peyton Rous, a youthful

---

### PROFESSOR HAROLD E. VARMUS
### ACCEPTANCE REMARKS (excerpt)

The literature of my native tongue had its beginnings in your traditional stories, set down in Anglo-Saxon, a language descended from yours, and ancestral to mine. One of the great remnants of this early work, the epic poem *Beowulf*, teaches the importance of the great halls of Scandinavia during the harsh lives endured more than a thousand years ago—how the concentration of light, warmth, and vitality within those buildings offered comfort against the winter's darkness, the cold, and the constant threat of death.

The halls were physically magnificent and welcome sights for weary voyagers:

Briskly the men went
marching together, making out at last
the ample eaves adorned with gold:
to earth's men the most glorious
of houses under heaven, the home of the king;
its radiance lighted the lands of the world.

We read also about the delights within these halls: the joyous fellowship; the story-telling and the songs; the food, wine, and mead passed around. Gifts of gold and crafts were lavished upon visitors from afar and upon those bold in battle with dreaded monsters, like Grendel and his mother.

In these festivities tonight in your Blue Hall, we honor the vitality of this great tradition, not just the few of us fortunate to receive its bounty. For those whose exploits are being sung here, Grendel is a symbol for other dangers (as doubtless he has always been): for disease and ignorance, for human greed and brutality. As Mike Bishop and I listen to your praise and music, accept your art and gold, and enjoy your food, drink, and good company, we recognize that, unlike Beowulf at the hall of Hrothgar, we have not slain our enemy, the cancer cell, or figuratively torn the limbs from his body. In our adventures, we have only seen our monster more clearly and described his scales and fangs in new ways—ways that reveal a cancer cell to be, like Grendel, a distorted version of our normal selves. May this new vision and the spirit of tonight's festivities inspire our band of biological warriors to inflict much greater wounds tomorrow.

Michael Bishop and his laboratory colleagues.

Rockefeller Institute scientist who was so ridiculed that he abandoned the research. Later, other scientists recognized it, and he received the Nobel Prize at the age of eighty-six.

"We didn't set out to do the experiment or ask the questions that led to the prize," Bishop recalls. "We just sort of staggered into it, I guess you'd say. We became intrigued with the Rous sarcoma virus and the conversion of cells into cancerous growth. You could watch this happen in a test tube, and you'd say to yourself, 'My God, that's amazing! If we could figure out how that happens, we'd know something about cancer. Even though it's a chicken virus, and the tumors are in chickens, surely we'd learn

something about cancer in humans.' We began to wonder why the virus had this capability in the first place, when it wasn't essential to the virus. Peter Vogt, then at the University of Washington, had shown very clearly that the capability to cause conversion could be lost and have no effect on the ability of the virus to grow. The Rous sarcoma virus had a gene that caused cancer but had no other role. Where did the gene come from? Why did the virus have it when it didn't need it?"

Varmus had worked at NIH developing molecular probes. Aided by research by Vogt, he devised a highly sophisticated technique to look at a single DNA molecule within the cell. The researcher Dominique

*V*armus and Bishop arrive at the Karolinska Institute.

Stehelin, visiting from France, used the probe to locate quickly the gene within the virus that caused cancer. They named it the Sarc gene because the virus induced sarcomas, a form of cancer, in chickens. (Later, the term was shortened to src, still pronounced "Sarc.") Then they began to use their probe to look for the gene elsewhere.

"And lo and behold," says Bishop, "we could find the same gene in normal cells. First we found it in chicken DNA, and then we looked across all different kinds of birds, including the most primitive we could get our hands on, an emu. And everywhere we looked we found it. At first we couldn't find it anywhere else, but then another postdoctoral fellow, Deborah Spector, by a technical tour de force, showed that there seemed to be something similar even in human cells. Why, we even found it in sea urchins!

"That immediately told us that the gene used by the retrovirus to grow and proliferate and the cancer gene had separate origins, and that the cancer gene had an origin in the distant past of evolution, since it had been conserved over millions of years. Suddenly we realized just from an evolutionary argument alone that the cancer gene was a cellular gene, not a viral gene at all. And that turned the Huebner-Todaro theory on its head. It said, 'No, this is not a viral gene that's being activated; it's actually a cellular gene that the viruses have got by accident by a sort of piracy during their proliferation in the cell.'

"And the next leap of faith, which we actually put into the last sentence of the first paper we published, was to suggest that there were probably multiple genes of this sort in cells and that they might represent the genetic vehicle for cancer even when viruses were not present. They were obviously not there just to cause tumors. They normally perform important functions but, if perturbed by carcinogens, could become cancer genes. And that's the theory that eventually played out and led to the recognition by the Nobel Committee."

Although Bishop sums their research up easily, it actually spanned nearly six years. Neither he nor Varmus can recall a moment when they suddenly recognized that they had come across something important, a landmark discovery. Instead, they remember that the Hubner-Todaro oncogene theory unraveled gradually. They were working very hard, both recall, in an atmosphere of great excitement, to the detriment and dismay of their families. Kathryn Bishop once told an interviewer that during this period, despairing of the inroads his work made on their relationship, she suggested they see a marriage counselor. Her husband suggested she go alone, because his schedule was too crowded.

When their first report was published in *Nature*, it was not greeted with what Varmus calls "incredible enthusiasm." Indeed, reviews were decidedly mixed. On the one hand, many other researchers entered the field and confirmed the UCSF results. Others did not relinquish dogma so easily. One group of critics, for instance, scoffed that all the two men had shown was that a cancer-causing gene existed in chickens; what had that to do with cancer in mammals and, more particularly, human beings? A second declared that the discovery had not been shown to be related to cancer, that it was just a fluke of the viruses. Indeed, it was not for several years, until new techniques made it possible to clone the src gene, that their findings were fully accepted.

Ironically, the src gene established the paradigm for the genesis of cancer, yet it has never been implicated in any form of human cancer. So Bishop began looking at another virus, known as MC-29, which in chickens caused carcinoma, the most common form of cancer in humans. His own and other laboratories quickly showed that MC-29 had an oncogene of its own. Then UCSF and Stehelin's group in France worked in parallel to discover that the gene, called myc, was present in normal cells. And, Bishop says, "everywhere we looked we could find it— chickens, humans, everywhere. And we realized we had a universal on our hands." In fact, myc has since been implicated in many

*Professor Varmus hard at work in his laboratory.*

human cancers, including lymphomas and certain types of lung cancer. Since then, more than twenty oncogenes have been identified, each with its viral counterpart, and prevailing theory holds that disruption of the genes, transforming them into oncogenes, is the basis of all cancer.

Of course, the Varmus-Bishop story so far lacks a happy ending. For all the headline-making research that has followed their prize-winning discoveries, cancer still claims half a million lives a year in the United States alone; more than a million new cases are diagnosed annually. Nor, as the two men acknowledge, has their work yet led to great advances in treatment. The cure rate for major forms of cancer is about where it was ten years ago. "The cell is no longer a black box," Bishop reflects, "but there are only a few windows through which any light is falling."

And although the application to cancer has received the most attention, many scientists believe that the greatest Varmus-Bishop contribution was in basic understanding of the cell. Thanks to their work, researchers have gained knowledge about how the genes are involved in cell proliferation and differentiation. Other scientists have painted a fuller picture of the oncogenes, especially what are now called proto-oncogenes, genes that may develop into oncogenes, and of suppressor genes, which, for example, may halt a cellular action once growth or another process has been achieved. "Intuitively," Varmus says, "it's obvious that the control of cell growth will involve not only things that propel cells to grow but also those that retard growth. And you can just imagine that the

*Christopher Varmus, age 11, adjusts his dad's tie before the ceremony.*

same is true in cancer." Actually, genes that suppress tumor growth have already been discovered, and a hot field of research is now investigating their role in several forms of cancer, notably retinoblastoma, a cancer of the eye.

Meanwhile, the two laureates remain interested in oncogenes, but have also moved off in other directions. At present, they are not collaborating, and maintain separate laboratories. Bishop is director of the George W. Hooper Research Foundation, and Varmus is American Cancer Society Professor of Molecular Virology. Both are professors of microbiology, biochemistry, and biophysics.

Varmus has recently concentrated on viral research, including studies of the hepatatis virus and the human immunodeficiency virus (HIV), which is implicated in AIDS. He also has studied independently how retroviruses mutate genes within a cell. Bishop's particular interest has been in a study of fruit flies, whose genetics have been well documented, to explore the normal function of the proto-oncogenes. The two get together regularly, however. Twice a month, their two labs hold a "Rous lunch" at which lab members brief each other on the state of their research.

Neither expects the Nobel Prize to change their lives very much. They continue to teach as well as to supervise graduate students; Varmus spent a year's sabbatical working at a bench in his own lab and in David Baltimore's lab at MIT's Whitehead Institute.

Bishop is convinced that the Nobel Prize is particularly valuable in that it honors the individual. "Individuals make the glory of science," he says with passion. "If you look at the history of biomedical science, you can almost always trace things back to one or a few individuals, usually particularly courageous individuals who've taken on a problem that someone else wouldn't touch or taken a stance that's a little offbeat. Our field traces back to Temin, who for ten years was the subject of widespread derision because of his theory about how retroviruses work, but he was dead right. And it traces more distantly back to Peyton Rous, who made the first serious claim to have found a cancer virus,

and he was so widely ignored and derided that he dropped from the field eventually. So the creative individual makes the glory of biomedical science."

There is still room for creative individuals in biomedical science, the two men agree. Many questions remain unanswered. The normal function of proto-oncogenes remains a mystery. "Why do beings carry the src gene?" Bishop asks. "What does it do for them? And the parallel problem is, How does it do it? What's the biochemical function encoded by these genes? It's very important that we understand that, because if we're ever going to apply our knowledge of oncogenes to, let's say, the therapy of cancer, we must understand how the genes function so that we can design ways to intervene. There's obviously a large part of the script that hasn't been uncovered yet. It's written, but it's not uncovered.

"We've taken a major step in the journey toward understanding cancer, what it is and how it arises," Bishop says. "The great truth is that in order to control a disease completely you must first understand it. It's fair to say that when we understand how oncogenes are involved in human cancer, we will be on our way to important therapeutic devices, maybe even breakthroughs. And maybe even prevention. Cancer is a disease you'd like to prevent, not treat person by person, tumor by tumor. We could prevent a significant part of cancer if we could get cigarettes out of people's mouths."

With a slender smile and a shake of his head, the philosopher-scientist adds, "Nothing a molecular biologist is going to do will solve that problem!"

*Professor Lars Gyllensten, the Chairman of the Board of the Nobel Foundation, delivers the opening speech at the Prize presentation ceremony, beneath the watchful eye of Alfred Nobel (far right). Each year the Nobel Ceremony is held in the presence of the Swedish Royal Family, (top, from left) Princess Lillian, King Carl XVI Gustaf, Queen Sylvia and Prince Bertil. The laureates enter the stage in procession (above). Entertainment is provided from above the gallery (right).*

# THE PRIZE
# PRESENTATION
# CEREMONY

*The Nobel Prize laureate Dr. Camilo José Cela.*

# CHAPTER 6

# THE NOBEL PRIZE IN LITERATURE

## THE WORK OF DR. CAMILO JOSÉ CELA

*After the civil war was over and Spain had embarked on her many dreary years under the new regime, Cela made his debut. In high quarters there was a desire to see edifying books, preferably cheerful and sunny ones. Cela's first novel was about a multiple murderer who relates his life history before his execution. La familia de Pascual Duarte was printed secretly in a garage in Burgos in 1942, and by the time it had come to the authorities' notice the edition was almost sold out.*

**—Professor Knut Ahnlund**
Member of the Nobel Committee for Literature

A true man of letters better known for not behaving like one has been awarded the 1989 Nobel Prize for literature. At age seventy-three, Camilo José Cela is only a few years younger than Naguib Mahfouz, his immediate predecessor; he is also the first Spanish novelist ever to receive the award. In honoring an Arabic and a Spanish writer in succession, the Swedish Academy has by chance acknowledged the double ethnic role of the author of *Don Quixote*, the first modern novel. Cervantes would have smiled upon both awards, since it is to one Cide Hamete Benengeli, a Spanish Arab, that he attributes the adventures of Don Quixote and Sancho Panza. Spain's position at Europe's edge nearest Africa and the influence of Islamic culture on its history have contributed to the country's peculiar mixture of ancient traditions and restless originality. Cela exemplifies the best energies emerging from both tendencies.

Mastery of Castilian Spanish makes Cela (together with his predecessor José del Valle Inclán) the most original prose writer in the language since Cervantes. In Cela's hands, words behave like living entities; the world remains chaotic, unbearably harsh yet musical. In his fiction, joys and sorrows are endured as if they were in the shape in which a god might have created them. Besides his kinship with Cervantes, Cela reflects the influence of Spain's unique picaresque tradition. In the most important passage of his Nobel Lecture, he offers a memorable definition of picaresque candor:

> I write from solitude and I speak from solitude. Mateo Alemán in his *Guzmán de Alfarache* and Francis Bacon in his essay *Of Solitude*, both writing more or less at the same period, said that the man who seeks solitude has much of the beast in him. However, I did not seek solitude. I found it. And from my solitude I think, work, and live—and I believe that I write and speak with almost infinite composure and resignation.

In Hispanic culture, the word *soledad* implies more than mere loneliness or meditative study. As in the case of Gabriel García Márquez's great novel *One Hundred Years of Solitude*, the loneliness in *soledad* may involve blessed wretchedness and a higher awareness of sacred and profane realities. The person who endures *soledad* is naive in being wise, hopeful in accepting despair. In *soledad*, the world is viewed with a tragic sense of humor and extreme cynicism is rejected with elegance and noble pride.

Cela is best known for being hard on hope. His fiction is full of monsters, murders, and the awful habits of psychic and material hunger. Yet he is a writer primitively at odds with despair. In awarding him the Nobel Prize, the Swedish Academy has chosen a large mind set against moral certainties and polite notions of human freedom; it has

*The laureate receiving the Prize in Literature.*

praised the fury and dark beauty of the Iberian soul. Like Goya's paintings, Cela's fictions represent a skirmish in Spain's ongoing war with modernity.

Camilo José Cela Trulock was born on May 11, 1916, at Iria-Flavia, a town in Galicia, Spain's northwestern region. Although born in Santiago de Compostela, his mother was of English-Italian descent; his father came from a large middle-class family. The boy grew up in Madrid, where he received a Catholic education that included some training under the Jesuits. As he approached the age of twenty during the short-lived Spanish Republic, Cela studied medicine and had contacts with left-wing intellectuals, such as the poets Pedro Salinas and Pablo Neruda, and the great lyricist and playwright Federico García Lorca. Cela started as a surrealist, although like most Spaniards, his surreal vision lies within a native strain of expressionistic rebelliousness rather than within any given aesthetic method. His first published poem ("Amor inmenso") appeared in 1935. Franco's uprising against the Republic in July 1936 caught the young poet in Madrid.

During the next three years, Cela fought on the Nationalist side of the rebellion led by Franco. In October 1937 he began service in the infantry but was soon discharged as unfit for duty. Early in 1938 he requested entrance into the national police in charge of surveillance and security, with the express wish to be stationed in Madrid. Cela's detractors have never forgotten his role in the Falange's ranks, nor have the Falangists themselves neglected to exploit his youthful eagerness to enter the secret police, as when they made his request public in order to embarrass him upon his nomination to the senate in 1977, after Spain's return to democracy.

Readers from the United States may regard Spain's civil war as terribly familiar by just imagining their own war of secession and the one fought in Vietnam combined into one great struggle taking place on American soil. In spite of its richness and diversity, Cela's enormous output seems fixed on the civil war. He began to write fiction in the early forties with the war and its aftermath locked within his own grasp of reality. Almost thirty years later, in *San Camilo* (1969), he went back to the eve of the war and dedicated the novel to all the dead

*Cela arrives at the festivities with H.R.H. Infanta Dona Cristina, left, representing the Spanish Royal Family.*

young warriors. With this gesture against political partisanship and nationalistic ideologies, he dedicated the novel thus:

> To the lads on standby in 1937, all of whom lost something, be it life, freedom, illusion, hope, decency.
>
> And not to the foreign adventurers, both Fascists and Marxists, who glutted themselves killing Spaniards like rabbits, and to whom nobody ever gave a candle to hold at our own funeral.

But, in embracing his nation below the belt of political doctrine, Cela failed to assuage the liberals' anger against him. As shown in *Mazurca para dos muertos* (1983), his best fiction dwells at the heart of universal strife. If the war had not taken place, Cela would have found its fierceness beneath the soil on which he places the living and the dead, as if they were eternally droning a chant to memory, to the ancestral earthliness of being. It is the genius in the salt of the earth—the sense of being homeless though at home—that fascinates him and disturbs his liberal detractors.

Early in 1938 Cela published his second poem, "Himno a la muerte" ("Hymn to Death") in the review *Fábula*. Between 1940 and 1941 he held a variety of small jobs and began law studies but soon dropped them. Spain was living its darkest hour of hunger and revenge after a war in which a million people may have perished. Cela started to work on the novel that would bring him fame (*La familia de Pascual Duarte*) in 1940. The harsh realities of the post–civil war years nurtured his imagination; his vision of

the war cannot be separated from the unheroic scavenging that followed it. Upon falling ill with pulmonary tuberculosis in 1941, Cela turned to the classics and found his novelistic vocation; he was soon rewarded with success—and hostile noises—by the publication of *Pascual Duarte* in 1942. At age twenty-six, Cela became notorious in war-ravaged Madrid, and by age thirty, he had married, fathered a son, and published two more novels: *Pabellón de reposo* (1943), a dense and kaleidoscopic tale of illness and death in a sanatorium, no doubt influenced by Thomas Mann's *The Magic Mountain*, and *Nuevas andanzas y desventuras del Lazarillo de Tormes* (1944), perhaps less significant as a retelling of the wanderings and misadventures of Spain's best-known rogue than as

*Camilo Cela photographed in Madrid, May 1955.*

*Camilo José Cela and Her Majesty, Queen Sylvia.*

Cela's first effort in travel literature, a genre in which he would excel beginning with *Viaje a la Alcarria* (1948).

The size and variety of Cela's output are often ignored in discussions of his four landmark novels: *Pascual Duarte* (1942), *La colmena*, or *The Hive* (1951), *San Camilo* (1969), and *Mazurca para dos muertos*, or *Mazurka for a Dead Twosome* (1983). Such crass reduction of a major and magnanimous body of work has created in some the absurd view that Cela's best writing belongs to the forties and fifties. Yet, minor Cela includes treasurable things, among them some of the century's best travel literature.

The same type of chronicle that Lawrence Durrell and V. S. Naipaul have made into art while journeying abroad Cela has devoted to Spain's countryside, to its neglected regions and ancient local types. He likes the quick portrait: "something like a bittersweet sketch, halfway between caricature and watercolor . . . dealing with a given type or slice of life peculiar to what geographers almost poetically call arid Spain." He calls his journey to Alcarria's culturally remote land of honey a "libro antiguo," by which he implies the traveler's age-old standards: "truthfulness, simplicity, and the delighted witnessing of the unforeseen." Cela's sensibility is nomadic; it thrives in *vagabundaje*, in the sporadic desertion of civic routines in favor of wandering through hinterland with no settled goal in sight, as if in protest against the world's present course.

The misbehaving man of letters at large in Cela's graphic Madrid evokes the youthful James Boswell during his early London days (and nights), roaming after sundown across St. James's Park, transacting with ladies of the town in dark side streets and alleyways. Cela's bizarre slang orgy of 1964, *Izas, rabizas*

> ### CAMILO JOSÉ CELA
> ### ACCEPTANCE REMARKS (excerpt)
>
> The Swedish Academy is honoring me by inscribing my name in the margins of the roll of illustrious personages of contemporary world literature. It is an honor which is out of all proportion to my skill and ability. Apart from showing my gratitude with all my heart, I would like to be permitted to make clear that, if I have dared to arrive where I am now, it is only because I understand that that Prize is not just being awarded to me, but also to my contemporaries who write in the glorious language which is our tool: Spanish. I do not wish to dwell on this very sincere confession for, since my teacher has been Miguel de Cervantes, I know full well that an argument, however good, does not seem so successful when propounded at length.
>
> When on my way to Stockholm, in response to your benevolence, I asked myself about the reasons which brought me here. I surmised that your purpose was to reward the occupation rather than the person. If so, you have not erred, for, according to Cervantes, the goal of literature is to give justice its rightful place by rendering to everyone what is his, and by understanding and upholding good laws. Literature is hazardously and irreversibly my life, my death and my suffering, my vocation and my servitude, my constant yearning and my well-merited consolation. How peaceful my conscience becomes after I have said this!

*y colipoterras* (which translates as something like "Jades, Wagtails, and Strumpets"), offers a merciless commentary on a photographic gallery of Madrid prostitutes; as such, it embodies his voraciousness in recording the sham and bravura of filth and the words that sexual mimicry and life's oldest predatory business have left in their wake. All the joy that Dickens put to use in debunking jargons and the middling professions Cela devotes to serious lexicography. His *Secret Dictionary* and *Encyclopedia of Eroticism* defeat curiosity and render humor speechless; they seem like parodies of legal codes rather than instruments aimed against hypocrisy.

The need to adapt to censorship under Franco may account for the incidental character of Cela's work during the fifties and most of the sixties. He failed in efforts to have *La colmena* published in Spain. The novel circulated illegally in the country after its publication in Buenos Aires and had an enormous impact among Spanish critics. The author of the two most influential novels of the postwar period continued writing at a relentless and varied pace. In 1956 Cela founded *Papeles de Son Armadans*, a literary review elegantly framed in his peculiar aesthetics of the old and the new, in which a cult of the vernacular prevails over avant-garde experiment. With his election a year later to the Royal Academy, Cela became (at age forty-one) the youngest member of Spain's highest cultural institution.

Around this time, Cela's novelistic art seems to have fallen behind his celebrity as a man of letters. His detractors saw in *Pascual Duarte* and *La colmena* achievements limited by Spain's relapse after the Republic's failure to modernize the country along democratic lines; and those who saw in Cela the greatest Spanish writer since Valle Inclán felt that he kept squandering his talents in minor genres and the duties of fame. At a time when existentialism was fashionable and writers like Camus, Sartre, and Beckett enjoyed their widest recognition, Cela lived in Palma de Mallorca under the sun and in blood-and-honey twilights. As remembered by James Liddy, the island echoed with the mockingbird's romance in Cela's voice; he ruled like a younger Prospero over a terraced landscape harvested by tourists, resident poets, and painters. Being able to play host to life's random eccentricities coolly and without giddiness defines a style of virile charisma tinged with a dandy's theatrical elegance. Like his friend Picasso, Cela might say, "Je ne suis pas un *gentleman*," thus expressing a certain haste in the art of being alive, as a bullfighter might while elegantly moving away with his back toward the beast.

While gentlemen might be defined by the quality of their respect for ladies and their own mothers, those who reject the label might excel in adopting a female persona in a style of borrowed madness. Although the way into Cela's fiction usually begins with the confessions of Pascual Duarte (a brutal peasant who killed his own mother), the

*Dancing as deftly as he writes, Cela draws the attention of the Banquet Hall.*

reader may well begin at the opposite end of the spectrum, with the letters that Mrs. Caldwell writes to her drowned son. In *Mrs. Caldwell habla con su hijo* (1953), Cela pays homage to a mother's incestuous love for the only kind of lover she finds among men, her own transfigured son.

By allowing political issues to dominate our understanding of Cela's fiction, we may neglect what Henry James sought as the figure in the carpet, the artist's true, hidden face. For instance, though gruesomely political and crowded with all sorts of characters, *San Camilo* begins by fixing our eyes on Cela's face. It is the face of a son, from a photograph taken in 1936, a face of vertical beauty that leaps at the reader like a glowering mandrake with immense and somber eyes. Thus, Cela's imaginary biography may be found in the voice of an English mother who speaks Spanish to her vanished son-lover like a poet in mourning would, and in the photograph of a son whose novels carry a note of regret and fury for having survived a war among brothers.

From Goya's *Disasters of War* to Picasso's *Guernica*, the subject of Spain's greatest democratic art lies in its people's slaughter as they fight for freedom. With the exception of Miro's minimal shapes and childlike wisdom, the Spanish stamp in art is a mark of pain. Under the long moratorium imposed by Franco's rule, the country revealed its soul mainly through paintings and films produced elsewhere. While Franco's Spain was visited by legions of tourists, the true Spain was carried abroad by Picasso to France, by Dalí to Hollywood and New York, and by Buñuel to Mexico. As witnessed by these

artists (and by Stravinsky, Eliot, Pound, and Joyce), modernism was to a large extent a migration; it became as portable as the unconscious it tried to render visible.

In his own style, Cela follows the same modern pilgrimage but within the Iberian geography. Of all the great modernists, it is Joyce he most resembles, the more because he never imitates him (after all, Cela comes from Galicia, Spain's most Irish region). Like Joyce, Cela is an innovator even when he is following certain influences, like Dos Passos's cubist techniques or Sartre's clockwork realism; he is a master of primal voices, a philologist of the unconscious, a demon lifting roofs to spy on private doctrines and rites, a mythmaker of the unsung and trivial, an orphic streetwalker, a Whitman wearing a beret and expressing pantheistic fondness for eating well and shaking the tree of love.

Besides celebrating Cela's entire achievement, the Nobel Prize might help to free his reputation as a writer from its own past burdens. As much as he and his viewers may enjoy his current role as a television personality, such celebrity helps to place his now remote masterpieces among the extinct and mythic beings of the literary past. A revival of these works—including the relatively recent (1973) but awesomely archaic *Oficio de Tinieblas*—would be as welcome as the task of freeing them from older interpretations. Younger critics and newer audiences—presumably not susceptible to the embarrassments caused by Cela decades ago—could destroy old myths and help to create some fresh ones. Among the notions in need of revision is that of Cela's insularity and native thickness. It is time to accept

*Cela delivers the Nobel Lecture in Literature at the Swedish Academy.*

that, had he written in English, French, or even German, Cela's output between 1942 and the early seventies would have earned him the same recognition enjoyed by Mailer, Bellow, Grass, and other contemporary masters.

Whether or not Cela's vintage might have survived in other cultural climates is a matter of conjecture. Fortunately, his revival has been self-engendered, for during the past decade he has written his most original work since *Pascual Duarte*: in 1983 he published *Mazurca para dos muertos*, the first in what is to become a trilogy of novels set in rural Galicia. He is currently at work on the second part, *Madera de boj* (*Boxwood*). *Mazurca* is a story of clan revenge upon the killer of one of its members. It is a work built on inlaid voices and occasions, on names and persons resonant, buried and sowed in a land whose blood justice they protect like totems against drifters and intruders. The rural world that Cela is now creating evokes the lyrical naturalism of Thomas Hardy, broken and fragmented in the style of young Faulkner's layered vernaculars and dissonances.

Besides *Mazurca*, Cela published the first Spanish western, *Christo versus Arizona* (1985). Like England with the highlands of Scotland to its north, Spain had a frontier throughout its Middle Ages; on it Christians fought Moors for centuries, from Castile into Andalusia and North Africa. This tradition was transplanted to the New World, where it branched out from war and pillage into a search for cities built with gold. Cela went to Arizona prospecting for lives, for the awful breath and deeds of renegades and *pistoleros*. The result is a single two-hundred-and-thirty-eight-page paragraph centering on the O.K. Corral and mixing the acid humor of William Burroughs's *The Place of Dead Roads* with the fluctuations of tenderness and violence in Larry McMurtry's *Anything for Billy*.

Cela continues to anticipate and outlast his peers. Few contemporary writers can match his range, verbal richness, and purity of means. Few have given better evidence of dwelling in awfulness while caressing beauty. No other artist—except Picasso—has tapped such energies at the age when most gentlemen tend their gardens. Camilo José Cela approaches dusk with a steadfast gaze that only a few writers of genius can turn upon the face of chaos. The Nobel Parnassus must be trembling a bit, and more than a few arguments must be raging there. Spain should be happier—and wiser.

*His Holiness The Dalai Lama after receiving the 1989 Raoul Wallenberg Congressional Human Rights award.*

# CHAPTER 7

# THE NOBEL PRIZE IN PEACE

## THE WORK OF HIS HOLINESS TENZIN GYATSO THE 14TH DALAI LAMA OF TIBET

*This year's Nobel Peace Prize has been awarded to His Holiness The Dalai Lama, first and foremost for his consistent resistance to the use of violence in his people's struggle to regain their liberty. . . . We affirm our unstinting support for his work for peace, and for the unarmed masses on the march in many lands for liberty, peace, and human rights.*

—Egil Aarvik
Chairman of the Norwegian Nobel Committee

On October 5, 1989, shortly before three o'clock in the morning, the telephone rang in the house in Newport Beach, California, where the Dalai Lama—the exiled religious and political ruler of Tibet—was staying. It was the secretary of the Norwegian Nobel Committee in Oslo, calling to notify him that soon in Oslo it would be eleven o'clock and the official announcement would be made that the Dalai Lama had won the Nobel Peace Prize for 1989.

The Dalai Lama's staff did not want to interrupt his sleep or disturb him when he woke at his usual hour of four and proceeded with his devotions. The secretary of the No-bel Committee, unable to give the word personally to the Dalai Lama, sent off a cable. Soon the news would be out and received with great joy by communities of Tibetan exiles in India, Nepal, and elsewhere, but heard with anger in governmental circles in Beijing.

How did the Dalai Lama happen to be in Southern California? He was meeting with prominent American neuroscientists who were briefing him on their work on the mind-brain relationship, while he in return was explaining to them the Tibetan Buddhist techniques of meditation and its relevance to their study of sleep and dreaming.

The Dalai Lama next visited Buddhist

centers in Northern California. One morning he went by helicopter to the summit of Mt. Tamalpais, where in his traditional maroon-and-saffron robes he led Buddhist monks in an ancient Tibetan ceremony designed to create harmony between people and their environment. On a throne set up under a white tent next to the crumbling barracks of an abandoned Air Force radar station, the Dalai Lama prayed for environmental peace while the monks chanted, sounded their horns and cymbals, and a white plume of juniper smoke rose up to the sky.

The helicopter then took him to San Francisco, where he explained before twelve hundred luncheon guests his plan to make peace between China and the Tibetan people, who since 1948 have lived under Chinese occupation.

What kind of person is this Tibetan Buddhist who consorts with scientists and who helicopters between religious ceremonies and political speeches? He insists, "I am a simple Buddhist monk, nothing more." He is a good deal more, not only a world scholar and teacher of Buddhism, but to devout Tibetans the reincarnation of a being who is so enlightened that he could ascend to the highest spiritual state but instead, to serve his people, has returned again and again to take rebirth. In the person of Tenzin Gyatso, Tibetans believe, the Dalai Lama has come to them for the fourteenth time.

It is not accurate to describe the Dalai Lama as a god-king, as so many Western journalists do. Buddhism does not have the concept of a creator deity, as in Judeo-Christian belief. Other high-ranking Tibetan monks are also regarded as reincarnations, but the Dalai Lama is considered a more highly evolved being, an embodiment of the spirit of compassion.

Though venerated by his people, he is modest and unpretentious, wearing the same unadorned robes as other Buddhist monks. Ever cheerful, with an abundant fund of humor, his interviews are punctuated with frequent chuckles, and his smooth, round, bespectacled face is often lighted up with a smile.

He radiates the kindness he preaches, and his love for people is most evident. At the traditional torchlight procession in the laureate's honor at Oslo, the Dalai Lama stood

*Bertha von Suttner first inspired Alfred Nobel to consider the idea of a peace prize.*

*The Dalai Lama offers a traditional Buddhist scarf during a special prayer meeting in the Himalayan town of Dharamsala.*



on his hotel balcony to receive the homage of the crowd below. Before long, he descended to shake hands with as many as he could reach. At his Nobel Lecture the ceremony was delayed while he moved slowly down the aisle, joyfully greeting members of the audience at the end of each row.

In his forthcoming autobiography he recalls what it was like to have been "a country boy" who at the age of five was proclaimed Supreme Leader of six million people. When the thirteenth Dalai Lama died in 1933, the search began for the child in whom he had chosen to be reborn. Following signs and portents, the search party identified the two-year-old son of a farmer in northeastern Tibet. The child was renamed Tenzin Gyatso

and in 1940 installed in the capital city of Lhasa as the Dalai Lama ("Ocean of Wisdom"). While a regent ruled the country, he underwent a rigorous religious education and also studied secular subjects such as mathematics, geography, and English. His Western tutor has remarked upon his insistent inquisitiveness and his fondness for taking apart mechanical instruments like clocks and putting them back together again. At the age of twenty-five the Dalai Lama completed his education with the doctorate of Buddhist philosophy, passing the final oral examinations with the highest honors before a vast audience of monastic scholars.

Ten years before that, however, he had taken over the reins of government at the age of fifteen, several years earlier than usual, because of the political crisis resulting from the arrival of Chinese troops in Tibet. Tibet, a mountainous country about twice the size of Texas, is situated in the heart of Asia, between China and India. It has long remained geographically isolated, and its relationship with China has been uneven. When China has been strong, its rulers have treated Tibet as a part of their dominions. When China has been weak, as it was during almost four decades before the Commu-

---

### HIS HOLINESS TENZIN GYATSO THE 14TH DALAI LAMA OF TIBET
### NOBEL LECTURE (excerpt)

Today we are truly a global family. We feel a sense of sadness when children are starving in Eastern Africa. Similarly, we feel a sense of joy when a family is reunited after decades of separation by the Berlin Wall. But war or peace; the destruction or the protection of nature; the violation or promotion of human rights and democratic freedoms; poverty or material well-being; the lack of moral and spiritual values or their existence and development; and the breakdown or development of human understanding are not isolated phenomena that can be analyzed and tackled independently of one another.

Peace, in the absence of war, is of little value to someone who is dying of hunger or cold. It will not remove the pain of torture inflicted on a prisoner of conscience. It does not comfort those who have lost their loved ones in floods caused by senseless deforestation in a neighboring country. Peace can only last where human rights are respected, where the people are fed, and where individuals and nations are free. True peace with oneself and with the world around us can only be achieved through the development of mental peace.

Material progress is of course important for human advancement. In Tibet, we paid much too little attention to technological and economic development, and today we realize that this was a mistake. At the same time, material development without spiritual development can also cause serious problems. In some countries too much attention is paid to external things and very little importance is given to inner development. I believe both are important and must be developed side by side so as to achieve a good balance between them. Tibetans are always described by foreign visitors as being a happy, jovial people. This is part of our national character, formed by cultural and religious values that stress the importance of mental peace through the generation of love and kindness to all other living sentient beings, both human and animal. Inner peace is the key: if you have inner peace, the external problems do not affect your deep sense of peace and tranquility.

Clearly it is of great importance, therefore, to understand the interrelationship among these and other phenomena, and to approach and attempt to solve problems in a balanced way. Of course it is not easy. But it is of little benefit to try to solve one problem if doing so creates an equally serious new one. So we really have no alternative: we must develop a sense of universal responsibility not only in the geographic sense, but also in respect to the issues that confront our planet.

Responsibility does not only lie with the leaders of our countries. It lies with each of us individually. Peace, for example, starts within each one of us. When we have inner peace, we can be at peace with those around us. When our community is in a state of peace, it can share that peace with neighboring communities, and so on. What is important is that we each make a sincere effort to take our responsibility for each other and for the natural environment we live in seriously.

With the Cold War era apparently drawing to a close, people everywhere live with renewed hope. Sadly, the courageous efforts of the Chinese people to bring similar change to their country were brutally crushed last June. But their efforts too are a source of hope. I particularly admire the fact that these young people who have been taught that "power grows from the barrel of the gun" chose instead to use nonviolence as their weapon. These positive changes indicate that reason, courage, determination and the inextinguishable desire for freedom can ultimately win. In the struggle between forces of war, violence and oppression on the one hand, and peace, reason and freedom on the other, the latter are gaining the upper hand. This realization fills us Tibetans with hope that someday we too will once again be free.

The awarding of the Nobel Prize to me, a simple monk from Tibet, also fills us Tibetans with hope. It means that, despite the fact that we have not drawn attention to our plight by means of violence, we have not been forgotten. It also means that the values we cherish, in particular our respect for all forms of life and the belief in the power of truth, are today recognized and encouraged. It is also a tribute to my mentor, Mahatma Gandhi, whose example is an inspiration to so many of us. This year's award is an indication that this sense of universal responsibility is developing. I am deeply touched by the sincere concern shown by so many people for the suffering of the people of Tibet. That is a source of hope not only for us Tibetans, but for all oppressed peoples.

In conclusion, let me share with you a short prayer which gives me great inspiration and determination:

For as long as space endures,
And for as long as living beings remain,
Until then may I, too, abide
To dispel the misery of the world.

nists took power in 1949, Tibetans have gone their own way. In 1950, for reasons both geopolitical and ideological, the Chinese government denied the Tibetan claim of independence and moved to integrate the Tibetans into "the big family of the motherland." This meant extending Chinese military power across Asia and at the same time reforming the rigid, traditional society of Tibet, whose people were to be "liberated" from their servitude to the priestly and aristocratic classes.

During the next nine years, the young Dalai Lama tried to cooperate with the Chinese while preserving the cultural and religious heritage of his country. But Tibetan resistance to Chinese policies grew, and de-

spite all the efforts of the Dalai Lama to keep peace, rioting broke out and in 1959 spread to Lhasa. As the Chinese prepared to use armed force to establish order, the Dalai Lama, recognizing that any hope for Tibet's future rested with him, reluctantly escaped across the mountains to India, where he was given asylum.

After crushing the uprising, the Chinese proceeded with the sinification of Tibet. More than one-half of Tibet's original territory has been incorporated into the contiguous Chinese provinces, leaving only central and part of eastern Tibet to form the so-called Tibetan Autonomous Region. Massive Chinese immigration has been set in motion, making the Tibetans an under-

*His Holiness greets a child.*

*The Dalai Lama in prayer.*



privileged minority in their own territories. Their culture and its religious foundation have been undermined, most of the monasteries destroyed, and ancient treasures removed. Many of the brightest twelve- to fourteen-year-olds have been sent to schools in far-off Chinese cities, to be indoctrinated and trained to join Tibetan Communist Party cadres back home. China has made Tibet an important military outpost, with a large contingent of the People's Liberation Army permanently stationed there and strong nuclear missile bases. Tibet's natural resources have been exploited, and there are indications that it may become a major depository of nuclear waste.

An estimated one million or more Tibetans have died as a direct result of the Chinese occupation. Many thousands of religious and political prisoners have filled the jails and labor camps, and the widespread use of torture has been well documented. Yet, demonstrations in favor of Tibetan freedom continue, and the Chinese have had to declare martial law and close Tibet to the international media. Tourists who have been permitted to enter the country report that the most appreciated gift they can give a Tibetan is a photograph of the Dalai Lama.

In the Himalayan city of Dharmsala in northwestern India, where about a hundred thousand Tibetans have followed the Dalai Lama into exile, he has established a small Tibet-in-exile. He has organized there a political administration, economic and relief projects for the refugees, and schools where pupils study not only their ancient culture but also English and modern subjects. Also at Dharmsala are a monastery, a temple, a library of Tibetan works and archives (including Buddhist scriptures), and a school for painting, music, and dance. It is the intention of the Dalai Lama both to preserve Tibetan culture and to modernize and liberalize it.

He has promulgated a democratic constitution and declared that in a self-governing Tibet he would relinquish his political power. Meanwhile, he has an important political role to play in pleading Tibet's case for self-determination before the world. India, sensitive to its relationship with China, has not formally recognized the Tibetan government-in-exile, nor, for similar reasons, has any other country. In the United States, the Dalai Lama has found support in Congress but not in the State Department, although before Communist China was recognized, the Central Intelligence Agency was sending material support to the Tibetan resistance and even training Tibetan guerrilla fighters in Colorado.

In his far-ranging travels in recent years the Dalai Lama has visited with two Popes and other religious leaders, seeking unity among the denominations. He has lectured

*Upon his return to New Delhi from Oslo, where he accepted the Nobel Prize in Peace, The Dalai Lama receives a traditional Hindu greeting from an Indian girl.*

at Harvard and other universities, engaged in Buddhist activities in many countries, and lobbied for Tibet with major political figures worldwide.

While denouncing China's oppression of the Tibetans, he has continued to seek a peaceful resolution of the conflict. He has never ceased to urge his people to avoid violence in their struggle, not only because of Buddhist principles but because, as he declared in 1988 after the Chinese troops had fired on a peaceful demonstration in Lhasa, "nonviolence is for us the only way. Quite patently, in our case violence would be tantamount to suicide."

In September 1987 the Dalai Lama announced a five-point peace plan before the Congressional Human Rights Caucus in Washington, D.C., calling for "the conversion of Tibet into a zone of peace, a sanctuary in which humanity and nature can live in harmony." He asked for "respect for human rights and democratic ideals, environmental protection, and a halt to the Chinese population transfer into Tibet." Finally, he called for earnest negotiations between the Chinese and the Tibetans, and in a June 1988 speech before the European Parliament in Strasbourg, France, he declared his willingness to recognize Tibet as a self-governing entity "in association with the People's Republic of China," which would remain responsible for Tibet's foreign policy and maintain defense forces in Tibet until a regional peace conference could arrange for Tibet's neutralization and demilitarization.

The Dalai Lama knew that many Tibetans would still insist on full independence; just as many, especially among the younger generation, rejected his counsel of nonviolence, but he felt that it was imperative to begin dialogue with the Chinese. There was no response from Beijing, however, and events in 1989 have left even less hope for negotiations. In March the Chinese declared martial law in Tibet, and in June in China the hard-liners took full control and brutally suppressed the student democratic movement.

It was the Chinese situation, however, that apparently brightened the Dalai Lama's prospects for the Peace Prize. In recent years the Nobel Committee had recognized champions of human rights, including Andrei Sakharov, Lech Walesa, and Desmond Tutu, declaring that true peace must be based on justice, and this year there were again strong candidates who worked for human rights by the methods of nonviolence. The Dalai Lama had been on the list of nominees for several years, but events in China drew fresh attention to the Chinese violation of Tibetan human rights. That a prize for the Dalai Lama would be seen as a sign of support for the Chinese student movement of Tiananmen Square might also have been on the minds of committee members. Moreover, with the Dalai Lama nonviolence was not just a policy but part of a philosophy of life based on concern for all sentient beings and for nature. The Dalai Lama has often spoken of how Mahatma Gandhi, the apostle of nonviolence, inspired him. Nobel Committee members have expressed their embarrassment at Gandhi's absence from their roll of honor, and the choice of the Dalai Lama has made it possible to pay tribute to Gandhi's memory.

In mid-September the committee members arrived at their decision and then kept their secret until the official announcement on October 5. The Dalai Lama was cited for his nonviolent struggle for the liberation of his people and for his philosophy of peace, based on "a great reverence for all things living and upon the concept of universal responsibility embracing all mankind as well as nature."

As was expected, the Chinese denounced the Nobel Committee, claiming interference in their internal affairs, and they attacked the Dalai Lama as "a political figure" who was seeking "to divide the mother country." To many in the Western media the political implications were more noteworthy than the award itself. Some called it a response to the events of Tiananmen Square, a slap in the face to China.

To the Dalai Lama the prize was something different. In his acceptance speech at Oslo, he declared, "I believe the prize is a recognition of the true value of altruism, love, compassion, and nonviolence which I try to practice, in accordance with the teachings of the Buddha and the great sages of India and Tibet." He went on to say, "The prize reaffirms our conviction that with truth, courage, and determination as our weapons, Tibet will be liberated."

He referred to his peace plan but spoke at greater length of his Buddhist philosophy of life. "Everyone can develop a good heart and a sense of universal responsibility with or without religion," he said. All religions pursue the same goals, "that of cultivating human goodness and bringing happiness to all human beings," and there is no contradiction between religion and science. At Newport Beach he made the remarkable statement that if Buddhism were to be found inconsistent with the findings of science, then Buddhism should change.

Optimistic as always, he declared "that the ancient values that have sustained mankind are today reaffirming themselves to prepare us for a kinder, happier twenty-first century."

At the press conference held in Oslo after he received the Peace Prize, the Dalai Lama was at his best, informal and buoyant. When asked whether he had ever considered that the search party for the Dalai Lama might have made a mistake, he replied with a smile, "Well, I think I have achieved something in the last forty years. If I am the wrong Dalai Lama, perhaps it doesn't matter."

What about the government officials who will not receive him? He is not troubled: "The politicians change; the Dalai Lama remains." He thinks that in China the present generation of leaders will pass on, and within five to ten years he will be able to negotiate with the next leaders. He has met with Chinese students who have fled abroad and is convinced that China cannot escape the spirit of freedom sweeping many parts of the world.

Whether the wrong Dalai Lama or not, he is a most remarkable human being. It has been said that there is sad irony in the fact that the Dalai Lama would probably not have received the Nobel Peace Prize if it had not been for the Chinese invasion of Tibet. There is greater irony in the fact that after his forced departure from Tibet he became a

Photo courtesy of the Office of Tibet

*His Holiness plays with the children.*

very different person from the remote priestly figure perched high in his palace of Potala, surrounded by lamas and aristocrats and seen by ordinary mortals only in ceremonial processions. In the past thirty years he has lived in the midst of his people at Dharmsala, and in his travels he has seen the world. His insistent inquisitiveness has led him to probe scientific theories, to confer with other religious leaders, to study democracy, and to learn how to become a practitioner of international diplomacy. Yet, he has remained "a simple Buddhist monk" in the dedicated practice of his religion.

The Norwegian Nobel Committee has done well in awarding the Dalai Lama the Peace Prize. There can be no real peace when human rights are trampled, and it is now far less likely that the cause of Tibet will be forgotten or dismissed as an internal affair of China. But this prize has also emphasized that true peace must have a spiritual foundation, and it has turned our attention to the Dalai Lama's message of love and compassion. If we can harken to this message, it will be in the realm of the spirit that the Dalai Lama will make his most enduring contribution to the peace of the world.

*Laureate Professor Trygve Haavelmo.*

# CHAPTER 8

# THE ALFRED NOBEL MEMORIAL PRIZE IN ECONOMIC SCIENCES

## THE WORK OF PROFESSOR TRYGVE HAAVELMO

*Conditions for scientific work in economics underwent radical change during the 1940s. Modern econometrics, based on probability theory, was established; economic theories and models could now be quantified and tested more consistently and systematically. And it was Trygve Haavelmo who initiated and provided the guidelines for this important methodological development in economics.*

**—Professor Bengt-Christer Ysander**
Member of the Prize Committee for the Alfred Nobel Memorial Prize in Economic Sciences

As a young graduate student in the 1940s, Trygve Haavelmo approached one of his professors, wishing to discuss a few of his own ideas about the then relatively new field of econometrics. "At the time," Haavelmo today recalls, "I thought I knew something about econometrics. I exposed some of my thinking on the subject to the professor. Instead of entering into a discussion with me, he gave me two or three numerical exercises to work out. He said he would talk to me when I had done the exercises. When I met him again, I had lost most of my illusions regarding the understanding of how to do econometrics."

This early collision with the complexity of econometrics, fortunately for future generations of economists, only served to intensify Haavelmo's interest. Today, almost fifty years later, Haavelmo's own contributions to econometrics have proven so essential, so fundamental to the progress of the discipline that they are almost taken for granted by the economists and economic policymakers throughout the world who use them in their everyday work. This applies equally to the Federal Reserve economist who uses econometrics to understand better the effect of interest rate changes on the economy as a whole and the economist commissioned by a corporation to study microeconomic problems such as the potential impact of a price change on the demand for a given commodity.

Haavelmo's econometric work in the early 1940s had a profound influence on the work of Lawrence Klein of the University of Pennsylvania, who won the 1980 Economics Prize for his contributions to econometrics, and Robert Solow of the Massachusetts Institute of Technology, the 1987 laureate, among many others. Making Haavelmo the 1989 laureate, Solow said when this year's winner was announced, "is like giving the Prize in Physics to Thomas Edison. You slap your forehead and wonder why they didn't do it sooner." So great, in fact, is Haavelmo's contribution to economics that Prize committee member Bengt-Christer Ysander calls it "the story of how economics was transformed from armchair instinct to empirical science."

Economics has long struggled to break the bonds of "armchair instinct," struggled to gain greater proximity to the certainties of a natural science whose findings can be tested empirically. Early economists such as Adam Smith and David Ricardo were widely viewed as social theorists rather than scientists, and economics itself was considered not a scientific discipline but merely the speculative study of man's interaction with money.

The development of econometrics is cited as a major chapter in the story of economics' systematic evolution from the subjectivity of the social sciences toward the empiricism of the natural sciences. Haavelmo himself is blunt in his assessment of economics prior to the advent of econometrics in the late 1920s; economics then, he says, was characterized by "lots of deep thoughts, but a lack of really useful quantitative results." Without econometrics, in his estimation, "the science of economics might not have reached beyond the stage of general talk."

What is econometrics? New York University economics professor James B. Ramsey describes it as a "bridge between theory and real life." Econometrics can be defined as a complex of mathematical and statistical techniques used to test the empirical validity of economic theories. Econometrics also can be used as a forecasting tool applied to a multitude of economic "what if" problems: What will happen to consumer spending if income declines? What happens to prices if the money supply increases?

According to the Royal Swedish Academy of Sciences, Trygve Haavelmo was awarded the Economics Prize for two path-breaking contributions to economics: first, "his clarification of the probability theory foundation of econometrics" and, second, "his analyses of simultaneous economic structures." Before Haavelmo, econometrics as a bridge between theory and real life was a highly tenuous structure, a shaky thing made of sticks that might get you from theory to reality . . . but then again might not. Sometimes, as Haavelmo notes in his Prize lecture, it could get you to a place that merely gave the illusion of reality. Referring to the difficulties confronted by early econometricians, he cites "the danger of drawing hasty conclusions about cause and effect from observed connections between two or more economic variables."

An example of the danger Haavelmo mentions is provided in *The Identification Problem in Econometrics*, by Professor Franklin M. Fisher, who recounts the following horrifying, yet supposedly true, story:

> There was once a cholera epidemic in Russia. The government, in an effort to stem the disease, sent doctors to the worst-affected areas. The peasants of the province of S—— discussed the situation and observed a very high correlation between the number of doctors in a given area and the incidence of cholera in that area [i.e., more doctors were observed in cholera areas than elsewhere]. Relying on this hard fact, they rose up and murdered their doctors.

Variations of this story are frequently used by economics professors to introduce students to what in economics is known as "the problem of identification."

Haavelmo today recalls one of his most influential mentors, the Norwegian economist Ragnar Frisch, warning his students against the horrific consequences of incorrect assumptions about cause and effect with a story about the high positive intercorrelation between the number of flies on the western coast of Norway and the number of tourists visiting the region (spurious conclusion: promote tourism by breeding more flies).

Haavelmo developed statistical methodologies that solved the identification problem (see box), thereby greatly reducing the

*H*aavelmo receives the Alfred Nobel Memorial Prize in Economics from His Majesty the King.

possibility of economic decisions based on equivalently spurious correlations. Pre-Haavelmo, for example, it might have been possible to conclude that inflation is caused by high interest rates just because high interest rates are present whenever a rise in the money supply creates inflation.

Haavelmo clarified and made it statistically possible to cope with what are known as "feedback relationships"—that is, economic phenomena that, in relation to other economic phenomena, act simultaneously upon each other as both cause and effect. A simple example involves income and spending. When consumers have high income, they spend a lot, and when they spend a lot, they generate economic activity, which in turn results in high income. Using this example, it could be said that Haavelmo

*Haavelmo amid the splendor of the Banquet Hall.*

started from the assumption that income doesn't cause consumption any more than consumption causes income, and proceeded to evolve mathematical structures (simultaneous equations) for econometric investigations that would clearly reflect this simultaneity.

Prior to Haavelmo's findings, econometric analyses assumed one-way causation relationships between variables that in fact were engaged in simultaneous causation relationships. The ability to account for cause and effect accurately via simultaneous equations made it easier to isolate, and so measure, the economic variables that constitute a given economic theory or relationship.

Haavelmo made it easier for economists to control the conditions of an experiment in a way that natural scientists often take for granted. Chemists, for example, can precisely regulate the conditions of most experiments by deciding exactly what goes in the test tube with what, when, and for how long. Economists have never been so lucky. The economist seeking to test the validity of an economic theory has for a laboratory only the real world—a place fraught with simultaneous causation among interdependent variables that often are extremely difficult to isolate, a place driven ultimately not by certain hard-and-fast laws, as in nature, but by human behavior, which is always subject to change and never precisely quantifiable.

In addition to developing simultaneous

equations that accurately account for feedback relationships, Haavelmo improved methods of incorporating the randomness of human behavior into economic theories in order to test these theories in a non-random manner that could yield valid conclusions about the real world. By formulating economic theories in terms not of theoretical absolutes but of a series of probabilities, Haavelmo showed how quantitative methods could be applied to draw stringent conclusions about randomly occurring data.

Its complexity might make econometrics seem an exercise in ivory-tower abstraction; increasingly, however, econometrics has tremendous significance for ordinary people. Haavelmo's interest in econometrics arose purely from a desire to strengthen the empirical foundations of economics, but econometrics today is used widely as a macro- and microeconomic forecasting tool. "Economists using econometrics," New York University's Ramsey has written, "are influencing politicians in policies that very much affect our livelihood, standard of living and way of life."

The more sophisticated recent econometric applications include monolithic macroeconometric models run on supercomputers. Such models often consist of hundreds, sometimes thousands, of variables and equations that make them difficult to describe. Perhaps the best example is the first full-scale model of the American economy, the Wharton model, created by Lawrence Klein and Arthur Goldberger of the University of Wisconsin. The Wharton model considers the following major components, or groupings of relationships: household expendi-

tures; business fixed investment, inventory investment, and residential construction; exports and imports; public expenditures and revenues (federal, state, and local); production and labor requirements; population and its participation in the labor force; price and wage rates; income payment; and money and interest rates.

Macroeconometric models of this size have a myriad of potential applications. For example, they can be used to help gauge the potential impact of a new economic development such as the approximately $20 billion cut in defense spending that is now likely, given current events in Eastern Europe. "We

> The field that I represent is one where recognition is particularly welcome and encouraging and for this reason: We are not used to being thanked for what we do. If we warn against an economic setback and get heard, the setback may not materialize and we are called pessimists. On the other hand, if we stick to polite academic modesty and do not get heard, the setback may come and we meet the usual verdict: Why did you not tell us? That is, heads you win, tails I lose. But for us there is only one conclusion that is tenable. We will continue to do our best. I bow my head in gratitude on behalf of my fellow economists and myself for the encouragement we have received here today.
>
> **Professor Trygve Haavelmo**
> ACCEPTANCE REMARKS (EXCERPT)

## THE IDENTIFICATION PROBLEM
## IN ECONOMICS

Trygve Haavelmo's Prize-winning contributions to economics as a science stem in large part from his having solved what economists call "the identification problem." In his book *Economic Forecasting—Models or Markets*, New York University economics professor James B. Ramsey defines "identification" as "the procedure by which relationships between two or more economic variables can be isolated from complex relations among large numbers of variables."

The identification problem arises from the fact that economists cannot control the conditions of their experiments in the way that natural scientists can. They cannot take the chemist's approach, in other words, and say, "Oh, well, now let's take this much supply and that much demand, and isolate the two together in this test tube and see what we get in terms of price." Further complicating matters is the dynamic of simultaneous causation. Quantity supplied, quantity demanded, and price do not have a direct, one-way causation effect upon each other: The quantities supplied and demanded together cause price and vice versa; they exist in a state of simultaneous causation where it is difficult to sort out what causes what, when, and under which kinds of conditions.

Suppose, for example, that you are a government policymaker who, for a variety of reasons, doesn't trust the markets to set reasonable prices for a basic commodity such as wheat. It is in your power to fix the price of wheat and you would like to know how to achieve optimum results. To accomplish this, you need to derive the demand curve—that is, attempt to determine the future demand, given different prices.

In the 1920s, when econometrics was in its infancy, such an inquiry could not have been completed with any hope of solid results. Had you tried, you might have derived the supply curve instead of the demand curve by mistake and not known the difference. Some of the earliest econometricians, in fact, made precisely this error in attempting to derive demand, given changing prices. D. Gale Johnson, professor of economics at the University of Chicago, explains their mistake this way: "They sometimes got a function that sloped upward, which no self-respecting demand curve should do (it should slope downward). In fact, what they were doing was tracing out the supply function over time without knowing it."

Haavelmo made it clear that it was necessary to isolate the factors affecting demand on the one side and those affecting supply on the other so as to determine with clarity how each influences a critical variable such as price. Although today this may sound simplistic, the work that went into it involves complex statistical theory; what may seem obvious now when simply stated was then a source of confusion to some of the best minds in economics.

Returning to the wheat example, picture the following graph: The vertical axis represents supply and demand. The horizontal axis represents price. The supply curve slopes upward (the higher the price, the more suppliers are likely to produce), and the demand curve downward (the lower the price, the more buyers are likely to buy). The point at which they intersect, of course, is the current market price—that is, the point of equilibrium where supply equals demand. On the graph, the supply curve and demand curve will be invisible based on what you know currently.

What you know currently is only the price, which appears as a single random point on the graph. But as a policymaker, you don't need to know where this point is anymore. The current price does not provide the solution to your problem. You must estimate the effect of future price changes, which requires determining with

precision the loci of the supply and demand curves. You might think you know where they are already because, according to economic theory, the demand curve should slope downward and the supply curve should slope upward. But theory isn't good enough. You are formulating policy, so you need to be certain that your test does not reflect unusual circumstances skewing the supply/demand relationship.

You need to be sure that you have identified the key relationships accurately. So you isolate supply in terms of an exogenous, independent variable, such as rainfall, which affects supply but does not affect demand. When you express supply in terms of rainfall, you get a clear slope and thus can plot demand clearly in terms of price. Rainfall affects the final outcome, but only through supply; therefore, it identifies the demand curve and allows the demand curve to be identified only in terms of price or other equation-solving variables. This highly simplistic example is solely for the sake of explanation. In real life, there are of course many conditioning variables on both sides, making the identification problem far more complex.

don't know yet what's going to happen with this peace dividend," explains Klein. "Will it be used to reduce the U.S. budget deficit? Or will it be directed toward Third World development? Will the slowdown in military spending result in a slowdown in the economy as a whole? And if the economy as a whole does slow down, how will this directly and indirectly affect things such as interest rates, money market borrowing and so forth? We don't know, so we need a Haavelmo-type model to analyze these different scenarios."

According to Klein, econometric models based on Haavelmo's work could have proved critical to our understanding of the causes behind the economic nightmare of the Great Depression. If such models had existed in the late 1920s, they might have helped to forecast the depression and certainly would have helped to orchestrate this country's attempts to extricate itself from it. For example, says Klein, without such models, "the New Deal never realized just how much input was needed."

Macroeconometric models, Klein further points out, can be used fairly precisely to determine lag distributions—that is, how the price of steel in January affects construction starts the following summer, or how interest rates in March affect new car production in June. Complex microeconometric models, meanwhile, are used routinely to analyze the attractiveness of certain types of investments or forecast the demand for a particular commodity. A typical example is an econometric model used to analyze the prepayment behavior of mortgage-backed securities. Insurance companies routinely use such models to determine the attractiveness and risk of mortgage-backed securities relative to other income-producing investments.

But in spite, or perhaps because, of their widespread use, econometric models are frequently ridiculed when forecasts derived from them prove inaccurate. "There are several problems connected with forecasting," Klein wrote in *On Econometric Models.* "First, economic data are rarely accurate and frequently must be revised. This means that the data used in building a model for forecasting may have been revised by the time the model is used for forecasting."

A recent example of how government data is subject to dramatic revision over time is the government's gross national product (GNP) estimates for the second quarter of 1986. On July 22, 1986, the government reported a rise in GNP of 1.1 percent; on July 24, 1987, the number was revised to a rise of only 0.6 percent; a year later, it was revised yet again to show a decline of 0.8 percent; and, according to yet another revision on July 27, 1989, GNP actually declined a full 1.8 percent in the second quarter of 1986.

Small wonder, given such data, that stories abound of dart boards and astrologers with better predictive track records than econometric models. Still, notes Klein, the models are improving all the time and, because they can be run on supercomputers, today it is possible to replicate and calculate the distribution of errors. Also, he adds, because the models now have been in use for some time, "benchmark data are available, since excellent records have been kept of forecasts and their departures from reality." The Wharton model, for example, has forecast records back to 1963.

Haavelmo himself perceived the benefits of econometrics not in terms of its predictive capabilities but as a way to strengthen the empirical foundations of economics and thereby enhance its pragmatic power. "Econometrics," he said in his Prize lecture, "makes it possible for people to understand better what their welfare depends on . . . of course some people say they don't want to be ruled by experts. But they misunderstand. It's better to be ruled—or at least influenced—by those who think they know something than by those who use force. I am greatly impressed by the level of economic discourse among politicians today. They talk in an economic language their forefathers would have failed to understand as recently as forty to fifty years ago."

A century ago, when Alfred Nobel made provision for the Nobel Prizes in his 1896 will, economics was not included. (The Bank of Sweden created the Alfred Nobel Memorial Prize in Economic Sciences long after Nobel's death, in 1968, to celebrate its tercentenary.) If Nobel had any opinion on economics at all, he probably considered it—as did most people at the turn of the century—as a vague new social science of uncertain potential.

Today, however, few would dispute the scientific foundations of economics, and Nobel doubtless would find much to applaud in Haavelmo's achievements in securing those foundations. What's more, Haavelmo pursued his work in a spirit consistent with Nobel's emphasis on benefiting mankind. "The basis of practically all our fundamental theories [in economics]," Haavelmo once said, "is the behavior of people. I have met many people in the natural sciences who share my feeling that we must learn how to live together. After all, what's the use if we can't learn to live together?"

Haavelmo is blunt in his opinions and unpretentious in the extreme. Upon being informed that he was the recipient of this year's Prize in Economics, an honor openly coveted by many of his peers, the Norwegian economist commented simply, "I do not believe in such prizes." He expressed the opinion that the prizes should go to younger men who need the money to continue new work. (He turns seventy-eight years old in 1990.) Never a glory-seeker, Haavelmo in recent years has rarely traveled or attended conferences. Nor is he concerned with image. Asked why he chose to study economics, he replies, "I am not one of those who had a grand plan since childhood. I can tell you very simply what made me start economics. It was in 1933. You could not get a job. It was less embarrassing to be a student."

But beneath Haavelmo's laconic, low-key presentation shines a powerful belief that economics has the potential to improve human lives. The bulk of his professional life has been spent evolving structures to overcome what he sees as the primary shortcoming of economics as a science—namely, that its relationships are governed by human behavior, which is subjective, chaotic, and virtually inexplicable using hard-and-fast rules.

Yet, paradoxically, while Haavelmo sees this as a hindrance of means, he welcomes it where ends are concerned. After all, human behavior is more susceptible to change than, for example, the behavior governing the relationships of electrons in atoms or the paths of the planets. "It is the hope of most people," Haavelmo said upon receiving this year's prize, "that a society does not have to remain forever the way it happens to be at present. We can do something to make it better. And societies have changed and are continuously being changed by various measures of economic policy."

W hile Nobel prizes in Physics, Chemistry, Physiology or Medicine and Literature are identical on the face, the reverse varies according to the institution awarding the prize, i.e.: The Royal Swedish Academy of Sciences (prizes in Physics and Chemistry); The Nobel Assembly at the Karolinska Institute (Physiology or Medicine) and The Swedish Academy (Literature). All medals are struck in 23-carat gold and measure about 2½ inches in diameter. The medal's thickness varies depending on the value of gold. Each is currently valued at approximately 20,000 Swedish Kronor.

**Physics and Chemistry**

*Nature in the features of a goddess resembling Isis emerges from the clouds and holds in her arms a cornucopia. The veil that covers her face is held up by the Genius of Science.*

**Physiology and Medicine**

*The Genius of Medicine holds an open book on her lap, gathering in a bowl the water welling out from a rock in order to allay a sick girl's thirst.*

**Literature**

*A young man sits under a laurel tree and, enchanted, listens to and writes the song of the Muse.*

### Peace

*Three men form a fraternal bond beneath the phrase
Pro pace et fraternitate gentium. The laureate's
name is engraved on the medal's edge.*

### Economics

*Crossed horns of plenty appear beneath a likeness of
Alfred Nobel. The North Star emblem of the Royal
Swedish Academy of Sciences appears on the back of
the medal.*

# LIST OF NOBEL LAUREATES 1901–1989

| Year | Physics | Chemistry | Physiology or Medicine | Literature | Peace |
| --- | --- | --- | --- | --- | --- |
| 1901 | W. C. Roñtgen (G) | J. H. van't Hoff (Nl) | E. A. von Behring (G) | Sully Prudhomme (F) | J. H. Dunant (Swi)<br>F. Passy (F) |
| 1902 | H. A. Lorentz (Nl)<br>P. Zeeman (Nl) | H. E. Fischer (G) | R. Ross (GB) | Theodor Mommsen (G) | E. Ducommun (Swi)<br>C. A. Gobat (Swi) |
| 1903 | A. H. Becquerel (F)<br>P. Curie (F)<br>M. Curie (F) | S. A. Arrhenius (Swe) | N. R. Finsen (D) | Bjørnstjerne Bjørnson (N) | W. R. Cremer (GB) |
| 1904 | J. W. S. Rayleigh (GB) | W. Ramsey (GB) | I. P. Pavlov (R) | Fredefic Mistral (F)<br>Jose´Echegaray (Sp) | Institute of International Law, Ghent |
| 1905 | P. E. A. Lenard (G) | J. F. W. A. von Baeyer (G) | R. Koch (G) | Henryk Sienkiewicz (Pol) | B. S. F. von Suttner (Au) |
| 1906 | J. J. Thomson (GB) | H. Moissan (F) | C. Golgi (I)<br>S. Ramoń y Cajal (Sp) | Giouse`Carducci (I) | T. Roosevelt (US) |
| 1907 | A. A. Michelson (US) | E. Buchner (G) | C. L. A. Laveran (F) | Rudyard Kipling (GB) | E. T. Moneta (I)<br>L. Renault (F) |
| 1908 | G. Lippman (F) | E. Rutherford (GB) | P. Ehrlich (G)<br>I. Mecñikov (R) | Rudolf Eucken (G) | K. P. Arnoldson (Swe)<br>F. Bajer (D) |
| 1909 | G. Marconi (I)<br>C. F. Braun (G) | W. Ostwald (G) | E. T. Kocher (Swi) | Selma Lagerlof (Swe) | A. M. F. Beernaert (B)<br>P. H. B. B. d'Estournelles de Constant (F) |
| 1910 | J. D. van der Waals (Nl) | O. Wallach (G) | A. Kossel (G) | Paul Heyse (G) | Permanent International Peace Bureau, Berne |
| 1911 | W. Wien (G) | M. Curie (F) | A. Gullstrand (Swe) | Maurice Maeterlinck (B) | T. M. C. Asser (Nl)<br>A. H. Fried (Au) |
| 1912 | N. G. Daleń (Swe) | V. Grignard (F)<br>P. Sabatier (F) | A. Carrel (US) | Gerhart Hauptmann (G) | E. Root (US) |
| 1913 | H. Kamerlingh-Onnes (Nl) | A. Werner (Swi) | C. R. Richet (F) | Rabindranath Tagore (In) | H. La Fontaine (B) |
| 1914 | M. von Laue (G) | T. W. Richards (US) | R. Bafañy (H) | Not awarded | Not awarded |
| 1915 | W. H. Bragg (GB)<br>W. L. Bragg (GB) | R. M. Willstatter (G) | Not awarded | Romain Rolland (F) | Not awarded |
| 1916 | Not awarded | Not awarded | Not awarded | Verner v. Heidenstam (Swe) | Not awarded |
| 1917 | C. G. Barkla (GB) | Not awarded | Not awarded | Karl Gjellerup (D)<br>Henrik Pontoppidan (D) | International Committee of the Red Cross, Geneva |
| 1918 | M. K. E. L. Planck (G) | F. Haber (G) | Not awarded | Not awarded | Not awarded |
| 1919 | J. Stark (G) | Not awarded | J. Bordet (B) | Carl Spitteler (Swi) | T. W. Wilson (US) |
| 1920 | C. E. Guillaume (F) | W. H. Nernst (G) | S. A. S. Krogh (D) | Knut Hamsun (N) | L. V. A. Bourgeois (F) |
| 1921 | A. Einstein (G/Swi) | F. Soddy (GB) | Not awarded | Anatole France (F) | K. H. Branting (Swe)<br>C. L. Lange (N) |
| 1922 | N. Bohr (D) | F. W. Aston (GB) | A. V. Hill (GB)<br>O. F. Meyerhof (G) | Jacinto Benavente (Sp) | F. Nansen (N) |
| 1923 | R. A. Millikan (US) | F. Pregl (Au) | F. G. Banting (Ca)<br>J. J. R. Macleod (Ca) | W. B. Yeats (Ir) | Not awarded |
| 1924 | K. M. G. Siegbahn (Swe) | Not awarded | W. Einthoven (Nl) | Wladyslaw Reymont (Pol) | Not awarded |
| 1925 | J. Franck (G)<br>G. Hertz (G) | R. A. Zsigmondy (G) | Not awarded | G. B. Shaw (GB) | J. A. Chamberlain (GB)<br>C. G. Dawes (US) |
| 1926 | J. B. Perrin (F) | T. Svedberg (Swe) | J. A. G. Fibiger (D) | Grazia Deledda (I) | A. Briand (F)<br>G. Stresemann (G) |
| 1927 | A. H. Compton (US)<br>C. T. R. Wilson (GB) | H. O. Wieland (G) | J. Wagner-Jauregg (Au) | Henri Bergson (F) | F. Buisson (F)<br>L. Quidde (G) |
| 1928 | O. W. Richardson (GB) | A. O. R. Windaus (G) | C. J. H. Nicolle (F) | Sigrid Undset (N) | Not awarded |
| 1929 | L.-V. de Broglie (F) | A. Harden (GB)<br>H. K. A. S. von Euler-Chelpin (Swe) | C. Eijkman (Nl)<br>F. G. Hopkins (GB) | Thomas Mann (G) | F. B. Kellog (US) |
| 1930 | C. V. Raman (In) | H. Fischer (G) | K. Landsteiner (Au) | Sinclair Lewis (US) | L. O. N. Soderblom (Swe) |
| 1931 | Not awarded | C. Bosch (G)<br>F. Bergius (G) | O. H. Warburg (G) | Erik Axel Karlfeldt (Swe) | J. Addams (US)<br>N. M. Butler (US) |
| 1932 | W. Heisenberg (G) | I. Langmuir (US) | C. S. Sherrington (GB)<br>E. D. Adrian (GB) | John Galsworthy (GB) | Not awarded |
| 1933 | E. Schrodinger (Au)<br>P. A. M. Dirac (GB) | Not awarded | T. H. Morgan (US) | Ivan Bunin (stateless) | N. R. L. Angell (GB) |
| 1934 | Not awarded | H. C. Urey (US) | G. H. Whipple (US)<br>W. P. Murphy (US)<br>G. R. Minot (US) | Luigi Pirandello (I) | A. Henderson (GB) |
| 1935 | J. Chadwick (GB) | F. Joliot (F)<br>I. Joliot-Curie (F) | H. Spemann (G) | Not awarded | C. von Ossietzky (G) |
| 1936 | V. F. Hess (Au)<br>C. D. Anderson (US) | P. J. W. Debye (Nl) | H. H. Dale (GB)<br>O. Loewi (Au) | Eugene O'Neill (US) | C. Saavedra Lamas (Ar) |
| 1937 | C. J. Davisson (US)<br>G. P. Thomson (GB) | W. N. Haworth (GB)<br>P. Karrer (Swi) | A. Szent-Gyoïgyi von Nagyrapolt (H) | Roger Martin du Gard (F) | E. A. R. G. Cecil (GB) |

| Year | Physics | Chemistry | Physiology or Medicine | Literature | Peace |
|---|---|---|---|---|---|
| 1938 | E. Fermi (I) | R. Kuhn (G) | C. J. F. Heymans (B) | Pearl Buck (US) | Nansen International Office for Refugees, Geneva |
| 1939 | E. O. Lawrence (US) | A. F. J. Butenandt (G) L. Ružička (Swi) | G. Domagk (G) | F. E. Sillanpää (Fi) | Not awarded |
| 1940 | Not awarded | Not awarded | Not awarded | Not awarded | Not awarded |
| 1941 | Not awarded | Not awarded | Not awarded | Not awarded | Not awarded |
| 1942 | Not awarded | Not awarded | Not awarded | Not awarded | Not awarded |
| 1943 | O. Stern (US) | G. de Hevesy (H) | E. A. Doisy (US) H. C. P. Dam (D) | Not awarded | Not awarded |
| 1944 | I. I. Rabi (US) | O. Hahn (G) | J. Erlanger (US) H. S. Gasser (US) | Johannes V. Jensen (D) | International Committee of the Red Cross, Geneva |
| 1945 | W. Pauli (Au) | A. I. Virtanen (Fi) | A. Fleming (GB) E. B. Chain (GB) H. W. Florey (GB) | Gabriela Mistral (Chile) | C. Hull (US) |
| 1946 | P. W. Bridgman (US) | J. B. Sumner (US) J. H. Northrop (US) W. M. Stanley (US) | H. J. Muller (US) | Hermann Hesse (Swi) | E. G. Balch (US) J. R. Mott (US) |
| 1947 | E. V. Appleton (GB) | R. Robinson (GB) | C. F. Cori (US) G. T. Cori (US) B. A. Houssay (Ar) | André Gide (F) | The Friends Service Council (GB) The American Friends Service Committee (US) |
| 1948 | P. M. S. Blackett (GB) | A. W. K. Tiselius (Swe) | P. H. Müller (Swi) | T. S. Eliot (GB) | Not awarded |
| 1949 | H. Yukawa (J) | W. F. Giauque (US) | A. C. de Abreu Freire Egas Moniz (Por) W. R. Hess (Swi) | William Faulkner (US) | J. Boyd Orr (GB) |
| 1950 | C. F. Powell (GB) | O. P. H. Diels (FRG) K. Alder (FRG) | P. S. Hench (US) E. C. Kendall (US) T. Reichstein (Swi) | Bertrand Russell (GB) | R. Bunche (US) |
| 1951 | J. D. Cockcroft (GB) E. T. S. Walton (Ir) | E. M. McMillan (US) G. T. Seaborg (US) | M. Theiler (SA) | Pär Lagerkvist (Swe) | L. Jouhaux (F) |
| 1952 | F. Bloch (US) E. M. Purcell (US) | A. J. P. Martin (GB) R. L. M. Synge (GB) | S. A. Waksman (US) | François Mauriac (F) | A. Schweitzer (F/G) |
| 1953 | F. Zernike (Nl) | H. Staudinger (FRG) | H. A. Krebs (GB) F. A. Lipmann (US) | Winston Churchill (GB) | G. C. Marshall (US) |
| 1954 | M. Born (GB) W. Bothe (FRG) | L. C. Pauling (US) | J. F. Enders (US) T. H. Weller (US) F. C. Robbins (US) | Ernest Hemingway (US) | Office of the United Nations' High Commissioner for Refugees, Geneva |
| 1955 | W. E. Lamb (US) P. Kusch (US) | V. du Vigneaud (US) | A. H. T. Theorell (Swe) | Halldór Laxness (Ic) | Not awarded |
| 1956 | W. Shockley (US) J. Bardeen (US) W. H. Brattain (US) | C. N. Hinshelwood (GB) N. N. Semenov (USSR) | A. F. Cournand (US) W. Forssmann (FRG) D. W. Richard Jr. (US) | J. R. Jiménez (Sp) | Not awarded |
| 1957 | C. N. Yang (China) T.-D. Lee (China) | A. R. Todd (GB) | D. Bovet (I) | Albert Camus (F) | L. B. Pearson (Ca) |
| 1958 | P. A. Čerenkov (USSR) I. M. Frank (USSR) I. J. Tamm (USSR) | F. Sanger (GB) | G. W. Beadle (US) E. L. Tatum (US) J. Lederberg (US) | Boris Pasternak (USSR) (declined the prize) | G. Pire (B) |
| 1959 | E. G. Segrè (US) O. Chamberlain (US) | J. Heyrovský (Cz) | S. Ochoa (US) A. Kornberg (US) | Salvatore Quasimodo (I) | P. J. Noel-Baker (GB) |
| 1960 | D. A. Glaser (US) | W. F. Libby (US) | F. M. Burnet (Austr) P. B. Medawar (GB) | Saint-John Perse (F) | A. J. Luthuli (SA) |
| 1961 | R. Hofstadter (US) R. L. Mössbauer (FRG) | M. Calvin (US) | G. von Bekesy (US) | Ivo Andric (Y) | D. H. A. C. Hammarskjöld (Swe) |
| 1962 | L. D. Landau (USSR) | M. F. Perutz (GB) J. C. Kendrew (GB) | F. H. C. Crick (GB) J. D. Watson (US) M. H. F. Wilkins (GB) | John Steinbeck (US) | L. C. Pauling (US) |
| 1963 | E. P. Wigner (US) M. Goeppert-Mayer (US) J. H. D. Jensen (FRG) | K. Ziegler (FRG) G. Natta (I) | J. C. Eccles (Austr) A. L. Hodgkin (GB) A. F. Huxley (GB) | Giorgos Seferis (Gr) | International Committee of the Red Cross, Geneva League of Red Cross Societies, Geneva |
| 1964 | Ch. H. Townes (US) N. G. Basov (USSR) A. M. Prochorov (USSR) | D. Crowfoot Hodgkin (GB) | K. Bloch (US) F. Lynen (FRG) | Jean-Paul Sartre (F) (declined the prize) | M. L. King (US) |
| 1965 | S.-I. Tomonaga (J) J. Schwinger (US) R. P. Feynman (US) | R. B. Woodward (US) | F. Jacob (F) A. Lwoff (F) J. Monod (F) | Mikhail Sholokhov (USSR) | United Nations' Children's Fund (UNICEF) |
| 1966 | A. Kastler (F) | R. S. Mulliken (US) | P. Rous (US) C. B. Huggins (US) | Shmuel Y. Agnon (Is) Nelly Sachs (G) | Not awarded |

| Year | Physics | Chemistry | Physiology or Medicine | Literature | Peace |
| --- | --- | --- | --- | --- | --- |
| 1967 | H. A. Bethe (US) | M. Eigen (FRG)<br>R. G. W. Norrish (GB)<br>G. Porter (GB) | R. Granit (Swe)<br>H. K. Hartline (US)<br>G. Wald (US) | Miguel A. Asturias (Guat) | Not awarded |
| 1968 | L. W. Alvarez (US) | L. Onsager (US) | R. W. Holley (US)<br>H. G. Khorana (US)<br>M. W. Nirenberg (US) | Yasunari Kawabata (J) | R. Cassin (F) |
| 1969 | M. Gell-Mann (US) | D. H. R. Barton (GB)<br>O. Hassel (N) | M. Delbrück (US)<br>A. D. Hershey (US)<br>S. E. Luria (US) | Samuel Beckett (Ir) | International Labour Organisation, Geneva |
| 1970 | H. Alfvén (Swe)<br>L. Néel (F) | L. Leloir (Ar) | B. Katz (GB)<br>U. von Euler (Swe)<br>J. Axelrod (US) | Alexander Solzhenitsyn (USSR) | N. E. Borlaug (US) |
| 1971 | D. Gabor (GB) | G. Herzberg (Ca) | E. W. Sutherland (US) | Pablo Neruda (Chile) | W. Brandt (FRG) |
| 1972 | J. Bardeen (US)<br>L. N. Cooper (US)<br>J. R. Schrieffer (US) | Ch. B. Anfinsen (US)<br>S. Moore (US)<br>W. H. Stein (US) | G. M. Edelman (US)<br>R. R. Porter (GB) | Heinrich Böll (FRG) | Not awarded |
| 1973 | L. Esaki (J)<br>I. Giaever (US)<br>B. D. Josephson (GB) | E. O. Fischer (FRG)<br>G. Wilkinson (GB) | K. von Frisch (FRG)<br>K. Lorenz (Au)<br>N. Tinbergen (GB) | Patrick White (Austr) | H. A. Kissinger (US)<br>Le Duc Tho (Vietnam)<br>(declined the prize) |
| 1974 | M. Ryle (GB)<br>A. Hewish (GB) | P. J. Flory (US) | A. Claude (B)<br>C. de Duve (B)<br>G. E. Palade (US) | Eyvind Johnson (Swe)<br>Harry Martinson (Swe) | S. MacBride (Ir)<br>E. Sato (J) |
| 1975 | A. Bohr (D)<br>B. Mottelson (D)<br>J. Rainwater (US) | J. W. Cornforth (GB)<br>V. Prelog (Swi) | D. Baltimore (US)<br>R. Dulbecco (US)<br>H. M. Temin (US) | Eugenio Montale (I) | A. Sakharov (USSR) |
| 1976 | B. Richter (US)<br>S. C. C. Ting (US) | W. N. Lipscomb (US) | B. S. Blumberg (US)<br>D. C. Gajdusek (US) | Saul Bellow (US) | M. Corrigan (GB)<br>B. Williams (GB) |
| 1977 | P. W. Anderson (US)<br>N. F. Mott (GB)<br>J. H. Van Vleck (US) | I. Prigogine (B) | R. Guillemin (US)<br>A. Schally (US)<br>R. Yalow (US) | Vicente Aleixandre (Sp) | Amnesty International |
| 1978 | P. L. Kapitsa (USSR)<br>A. A. Penzias (US)<br>R. W. Wilson (US) | P. Mitchell (GB) | W. Arber (Swi)<br>D. Nathans (US)<br>H. O. Smith (US) | Isaac B. Singer (US) | M. Begin (Is)<br>A. Sadat (Egypt) |
| 1979 | S. L. Glashow (US)<br>A. Salam (Pak)<br>S. Weinberg (US) | H. C. Brown (US)<br>G. Wittig (FRG) | A. M. Cormack (US)<br>G. N. Hounsfield (GB) | Odysseus Elytis (Gr) | Mother Teresa (In) |
| 1980 | J. W. Cronin (US)<br>V. L. Fitch (US) | P. Berg (US)<br>W. Gilbert (US)<br>F. Sanger (GB) | B. Benacerraf (US)<br>J. Dausset (US)<br>G. D. Snell (US) | Czesław Miłosz (Pol/US) | A. Perez Esquivel (Ar) |
| 1981 | N. Bloembergen (US)<br>A. L. Schawlow (US)<br>K. M. Siegbahn (Swe) | K. Fukui (J)<br>R. Hoffmann (US) | D. H. Hubel (US)<br>R. W. Sperry (US)<br>T. N. Wiesel (Swe) | Elias Canetti (GB) | Office of the United Nations' High Commissioner for Refugees, Geneva |
| 1982 | K. G. Wilson (US) | A. Klug (GB) | S. Bergström (Swe)<br>B. I. Samuelsson (Swe)<br>J. R. Vane (GB) | Gabriel García Márquez (Co) | A. Myrdal (Swe)<br>A. García Robles (M) |
| 1983 | S. Chandrasekhar (US)<br>W. A. Fowler (US) | H. Taube (US) | B. McClintock (US) | William Golding (GB) | L. Wałesa (Pol) |
| 1984 | C. Rubbia (I)<br>S. van der Meer (Nl) | B. Merrifield (US) | N. K. Jerne (D)<br>G. J. F. Köhler (FRG)<br>C. Milstein (GB/Ar) | Jaroslav Seifert (Cz) | D. Tutu (SA) |
| 1985 | K. von Klitzing (FRG) | H. A. Hauptman (US)<br>J. Karle (US) | M. S. Brown (US)<br>J. L. Goldstein (US) | Claude Simon (F) | Intern. Physicians for the Prevention of Nuclear War |
| 1986 | E. Ruska (FRG)<br>G. Binnig (FRG)<br>H. Rohrer (Swi) | D. R. Herschbach (US)<br>Y. T. Lee (US)<br>J. C. Polanyi (Ca) | S. Cohen (US)<br>R. Levi-Montalcini (I/US) | Wole Soyinka (Ni) | E. Wiesel (US) |
| 1987 | J. G. Bednorz (FRG)<br>K. A. Müller (Swi) | D. J. Cram (US)<br>J.-M. Lehn (F)<br>C. J. Pedersen (US) | S. Tonegawa (J) | Joseph Brodsky (US) | O. Arias Sánchez (CR) |
| 1988 | L. M. Lederman (US)<br>M. Schwartz (US)<br>J. Steinberger (US) | J. Deisenhofer (FRG)<br>R. Huber (FRG)<br>H. Michel (FRG) | J. W. Black (GB)<br>G. B. Elion (US)<br>G. H. Hitchings (US) | Naguib Mahfouz (E) | The United Nations Peace-Keeping Forces |
| 1989 | N. F. Ramsey (US)<br>H. G. Dehmelt (US)<br>W. Paul (FRG) | S. Altman (US/Ca)<br>T. R. Cech (US) | J. M. Bishop (US)<br>H. E. Varmus (US) | Camilo José Cela (Sp) | The 14th Dalai Lama (Tenzin Gyatso) (Tib) |

# THE BANK OF SWEDEN PRIZE IN ECONOMICS IN MEMORY OF ALFRED NOBEL, LIST OF LAUREATES

| | | | | | | | |
|---|---|---|---|---|---|---|---|
| 1969 | R. Frisch (N) | 1974 | G. Myrdal (Swe) | 1978 | H. Simon (US) | 1983 | G. Debreu (US) |
| | J. Tinbergen (Nl) | | F. A. von Hayek (GB) | 1979 | A. Lewis (GB) | 1984 | R. Stone (GB) |
| 1970 | P. Samuelson (US) | 1975 | L. V. Kantorovich (USSR) | | T. W. Schultz (US) | 1985 | F. Modigliani (US) |
| 1971 | S. Kuznets (US) | | T. C. Koopmans (US) | 1980 | L. Klein (US) | 1986 | J. M. Buchanan Jr. (US) |
| 1972 | J. R. Hicks (GB) | 1976 | M. Friedman (US) | 1981 | J. Tobin (US) | 1987 | R. M. Solow (US) |
| | K. Arrow (US) | 1977 | B. Ohlin (Swe) | 1982 | G. J. Stigler (US) | 1988 | M. Allais (F) |
| 1973 | W. Leontief (US) | | J. Meade (GB) | | | 1989 | T. Haavelmo (N) |

## Abbreviations

Ar Argentina; Austr Australia; Au Austria; B Belgium; Ca Canada; Co Colombia; CR Costa Rica; Cz Czechoslovakia; D Denmark; E Egypt; Fi Finland; F France; FRG Federal Republic of Germany; G Germany (before 1948); GB Great Britain; Gr Greece; Guat Guatemala; H Hungary; Ic Iceland; In India; Ir Ireland; Is Israel; I Italy; J Japan; M Mexico; Nl The Netherlands; Ni Nigeria; N Norway; Pak Pakistan; Pol Poland; Por Portugal; R Russia (after 1922 USSR); Sp Spain; Swe Sweden; Swi Switzerland; SA Republic of South Africa; Tib Tibet; US United States; Y Yugoslavia.

# IN MEMORIAM

*SAMUEL BECKETT, Ireland (1906–1989)*
*1969 Laureate in Literature*

---

*SIR JOHN R. HICKS, Great Britain (1904–1989)*
*1972 winner in Economic Sciences*

---

*KONRAD LORENZ, Austria (1903–1989)*
*1973 Laureate in Physiology or Medicine*

---

*CHARLES J. PEDERSEN, U.S.A. (1904–1989)*
*1987 Laureate in Chemistry*

---

*ANDREI SAKHAROV, U.S.S.R. (1921–1989)*
*1975 Laureate in Peace*

---

*EMILO GINO SEGRE, U.S.A. (1905–1989)*
*1959 Laureate in Physics*

---

*WILLIAM SHOCKLEY, U.S.A. (1910–1989)*
*1956 Laureate in Physics*

# ABOUT THE AUTHORS

### BARON STIG RAMEL

Stig Ramel has since 1972 been Executive Director of the Nobel Foundation. He was vice president, later president, of the General Swedish Export Association from 1966–1972 and is chairman, vice chairman or board member of eighteen Swedish and international companies and organizations. From 1953–1966, he represented the Swedish Embassy and Ministry for Foreign Affairs in Paris, Washington and elsewhere.

### WILHELM ODELBERG

Wilhelm Odelberg, Ph.D., is former head librarian of Stockholm University, a member of the Royal Swedish Academy of Sciences, and vice president of the Royal Academy of Military Sciences. He is author of several books and articles on modern history, biographies, and the history of science, and editor (1968–1988) of *Les Prix Nobel*, the yearbook of the Nobel Foundation.

### IRWIN ABRAMS

Irwin Abrams, author of *The Nobel Peace Prize and the Laureates* (1988), is the world's foremost historian of the Nobel Peace Prize. He is a prominent scholar and practitioner in the field of international education. A lifelong peace advocate, he participated in the world wartime relief and postwar reconstruction work of the American Friends Service Committee, joint winner of the 1947 Nobel Peace Prize.

### TOM ALEXANDER

Tom Alexander is a retired member of the board of editors of *Fortune*, where he was employed for 25 years. He has also written for *Saturday Evening Post*, *Life*, *TIME*, *Smithsonian*, *Popular Science* and other magazines, and is the author of two books: *Project Apollo: Man to the Moon* and, for TIME-Life Books' Computer Library, *Artificial Intelligence*.

### SHARON BEGLEY

Sharon Begley has been the science editor of *Newsweek* magazine since 1982, where she reports and writes on subjects ranging from astronomy to zoology, space science to science policy. She has also taught environmental reporting at the Columbia University Graduate School of Journalism.

## EDWIN KIESTER JR.

Edwin Kiester Jr. is a Palo Alto, Calif., based free-lancer who specializes in medicine and science. He is editor of *Better Homes & Gardens' New Family Medical Guide* and co-author, with his wife Sally, of *Better Homes & Gardens' New Baby Book*. He has also written for *Smithsonian, Reader's Digest, Discover, GEO, Science Digest* and other magazines.

## EDUARDO GONZÁLEZ

Eduardo González left his native Cuba at age 17. He did graduate work in literary studies at Indiana University and taught at Williams and Bennington colleges. He is the author of several books, including *La persona y el relato* (1985) and the recently finished *The Monstered Self*. A resident of Baltimore, he teaches literature at Johns Hopkins University and is currently at work on a book dealing with myth in fiction, film and comic strips.

## LIZ HECHT

Liz Hecht is a New York-based, free-lance writer. Her work has appeared in the *New York Times, New York Woman, Institutional Investor* and *City Sports*. She is currently at work on a book about sports obsession.